Don Carlos, Prince of Spain by Thomas Otway

Thomas Otway was born on March 3rd, 1652 at Trotton near Midhurst.

He was educated at Winchester College before entering Christ Church, Oxford, in 1669 as a commoner. For reasons unknown he left without a degree in 1672 but what is known is that Oxford create a passion in him for books.

Travelling to London that same year he met and obtained work as an actor from the playwright Aphra Behn. He was cast as the old king in her play, Forc'd Marriage but on his debut he had such a severe attack of stage fright that his acting career finished there and then.

His career now turned to writing plays and it was a career that was to prove of immense worth to the literary canon of England. In 1675, Otway's first play, Alcibiades was first performed. It is a tragedy, written in heroic verse, saved from absolute failure only by the actors.

In his play Don Carlos, Prince of Spain (1676) Otway made the leap to the front rank of playwrights and quickly followed it in 1677 with two plays adapted from French sources; Titus and Berenice, and the Cheats of Scapin followed in 1678 Otway by an original comedy, Friendship in Fashion, which continued his run of very successful plays.

In February 1680, the first of Otway's two tragic masterpieces, The Orphan, or The Unhappy Marriage, was performed followed by an indifferent comedy, The Soldier's Fortune (1681), and 1682 perhaps his best work, Venice Preserv'd, or A Plot Discover'd. The play won instant success.

However, in the last few years of his life poverty ensnared Otway. The success of his earlier plays had finished with Venice Preserv'd and the downward slope was both precipitous and destructive.

Thomas Otway, aged 33, died in the most awful poverty on April 14th, 1685 and was buried two days later on April 16th, in the churchyard of St. Clement Danes.

Index of Contents
INTRODUCTION
TO HIS ROYAL HIGHNESS THE DUKE
PREFACE
PROLOGUE
DRAMATIS PERSONÆ
SCENE—THE COURT OF SPAIN.
DON CARLOS, PRINCE OF SPAIN
ACT THE FIRST
SCENE I.—An Apartment in the Palace.
ACT THE SECOND
SCENE I.—An Orange Grove, Near the Palace.
ACT THE THIRD
SCENE I.—The Same.
ACT THE FOURTH
SCENE I.—The Ante-Chamber to the Queen's Apartment.
ACT THE FIFTH
SCENE I.—An Apartment in the Palace.

INTRODUCTION

Besides the writers mentioned in my Introduction, Campistron, a pupil of Racine, founded a play called Andronic on this same history of Don Carlos. Some Spanish historians, in the interest of Philip, have tried to blacken the character of his son. But the Abbé de San Real (who has been called the French Sallust) seems to have estimated him rightly, while the dramatists have, on the whole, adopted the Frenchman's conception, which was apparently derived from reliable Spanish sources. The motto prefixed from Horace is in allusion to the fact that this play received the approbation of the King and the Duke of York. It had a long success at the theatre, and we may agree with those who called it, as Otway tells us in the preface, the best "heroic" play of the time—containing, as it does, far less of rant and confusion, but more of nature and passion, than the "heroic" plays of Dryden—though Aurungzebe may not be far behind it. Booth, the actor, was informed by Betterton that Don Carlos continued for several years to attract larger audiences than The Orphan or Venice Preserved. It was first represented at the Duke's Theatre in the year 1676, and was published in the same year.

Philip II., son of the Emperor Charles V., became King of Naples and Sicily in 1554 on his father's abdication, and King Consort of England by his marriage with Mary two years after he ascended the Spanish throne. In 1557 he gained the victory of St. Quentin, which might have made him master of France, but he did not follow it up, being, it is said, so elated and yet terrified that he vowed: first, never to engage in another fight, and secondly, to found a monastery in honour of St. Lawrence at Escorial. Later came the great rebellion of the Low Countries, which, in spite of Alva's ability, sanguinary cruelty, and persecutions, resulted in the independence of "the United Provinces," and the triumph of the reformed faith. Philip subdued Portugal, and sent the huge Spanish Armada to conquer England, the illustrious heretic Elizabeth having succeeded to Mary. But the storms and the English together were too much for him. He showed resignation and dignity, however, when the admiral in command announced this misfortune to him. He married Elizabeth of Valois after Mary's death.

It is probable that Don Carlos inherited the personal pride and hauteur of his race, and he is said to have treated Alva with rudeness on a public occasion, only because the Duke was a little late in paying his respects to him. Alva, as a noble, had his share of pride, and being, moreover, malignant, never forgave this.

But the rivalry of these two personages in desiring the government of the revolted Netherlands is a more probable cause of the affront, for it seems to have been just before the Duke proceeded thither as Governor, when he went to take leave of Carlos, that it occurred. Philip had refused the post to his son, and given it to Alva. Carlos is even said by some to have threatened the Duke with his sword; but, if so, it seems likely that something in the words or triumphant demeanour of the latter provoked the hotheaded youth beyond endurance. This spirited and aspiring Prince was evidently far more liberal in religion and politics than his father, a disposition likely to be intensified by the fact that his father persistently kept him in tutelage, and forbade him all participation in the management of public affairs, which he so ardently coveted. That he entered into correspondence with the gallant men striving for liberty of conscience and nationality in the Low Countries seems certain. This was a pretext and motive for his arrest, imprisonment, and murder. But jealous suspicion that the Queen, promised and betrothed by Philip himself to his own son, cared too much for that son, and more than suspicion that Carlos cared too much for her, afforded a motive yet more powerful. Elizabeth of France (daughter of Henry II.) was put to death about the same time, and the Prince of Orange openly accused Philip of these murders, alleging that they were committed in order that he might be free to marry his own niece, Anne of Austria. Carlos is variously reported to have been killed by poison, strangulation, or opening his veins in a bath. Philip died in 1598. His character has been well suggested and outlined in a recent play, Lord Tennyson's "Queen Mary."

TO HIS ROYAL HIGHNESS THE DUKE [1]

Sir,

'Tis an approved opinion, there is not so unhappy a creature in the world as the man that wants ambition; for certainly he lives to very little use that only toils in the same round, and because he knows where he is, though in a dirty road, dares not venture on a smoother path for fear of being lost. That I am not the wretch I condemn, your Royal Highness may be sufficiently convinced, in that I durst presume to put this poem under your patronage. My motives to it were not ordinary: for besides my own propensity to take an opportunity of publishing the extreme devotion I owe your Royal Highness, the mighty encouragement I received from your approbation of it when presented on the stage was hint enough to let me know at whose feet it ought to be laid. Yet, whilst I do this, I am sensible the curious world will expect some panegyric on those heroic virtues which are throughout it so much admired. But, as they are a theme too great for my undertaking, so only to endeavour at the truth of them must, in the distance between my obscurity and their height, savour of a flattery, which in your Royal Highness's esteem I would not be thought guilty of; though in that part of them which relates to myself (viz., your favours showered on a thing so mean as I am) I know not how to be silent. For you were not only so indulgent as to bestow your praise on this, but even (beyond my hopes) to declare in favour of my first essay of this nature, and add yet the encouragement of your commands to go forward, when I had the honour to kiss your Royal Highness's hand, in token of your permission to make a dedication to you of the second. I must confess, and boast I am very proud of it; and it were enough to make me more, were I not sensible how far I am undeserving. Yet when I consider you never give your favours precipitately, but that it is a certain sign of some desert when you vouchsafe to promote, I, who have terminated my best hopes in it, should do wrong to your goodness, should I not let the world know my mind, as well as my condition, is raised by it. I am certain none that know your Royal Highness will disapprove my aspiring to the service of so great and so good a master; one who (as is apparent to all those who have the honour to be near you and know you by that title) never raised without merit, or discountenanced without justice. It is that, indeed, obliging severity which has in all men created an awful love and respect towards you; since in the firmness of your resolution the brave and good man is sure of you, whilst the ill-minded and malignant fears you. This I could not pass over; and I hope your Royal Highness will pardon it, since it is unaffectedly my zeal to you, who am in nothing so unfortunate, as that I have not a better opportunity to let you and the world know how much I am,

Your Royal Highness's
Most humble, most faithful, and most obedient Servant,
THOMAS OTWAY.

PREFACE

Reader,

'Tis not that I have any great affection to scribbling, that I pester thee with a preface; for, amongst friends, 'tis almost as poor a trade with poets, as it is with those that write hackney under attorneys; it will hardly keep us in ale and cheese. Honest Ariosto began to be sensible of it in his time, who makes his complaint to this purpose:

I pity those who in these latter days
Do write, when bounty hath shut up her gate:
Where day and night in vain good writers knock,
And for their labour oft have but a mock.

Thus I find it according to Sir John Harington's translation; had I understood Italian, I would have given it thee in the original, but that is not my talent; therefore to proceed: this Play was the second that ever I writ, or thought of writing. I must confess, I had often a titillation to poetry, but never durst venture on my muse, till I got her into a corner in the country; and then, like a bashful young lover, when I had her in private, I had courage to fumble, but never thought she would have produced anything; till at last, I know not how, ere I was aware, I found myself father of a dramatic birth, which I called Alcibiades; but I might, without offence to any person in the play, as well have called it Nebuchadnezzar; for my hero, to do him right, was none of that squeamish gentleman I make him, but would as little have boggled at the obliging the passion of a young and beautiful lady as I should myself, had I the same opportunities which I have given him. This I publish to antedate the objections some people may make against that play, who have been (and much good may it do them!) very severe, as they think, upon this. Whoever they are, I am sure I never disobliged them: nor have they (thank my good fortune) much injured me. In the meanwhile I forgive them, and, since I am out of the reach on't, leave them to chew the cud on their own venom. I am well satisfied I had the greatest party of men of wit and sense on my side; amongst which I can never enough acknowledge the unspeakable obligations I received from the Earl of R.,[2] who, far above what I am ever able to deserve from him, seemed almost to make it his business to establish it in the good opinion of the King and his Royal Highness; from both of whom I have since received confirmation of their good liking of it, and encouragement to proceed. And it is to him, I must in all gratitude confess, I owe the greatest part of my good success in this, and on whose indulgency I extremely build my hopes of a next. I dare not presume to take to myself what a great many, and those (I am sure) of good judgment too, have been so kind to afford me—viz., that it is the best heroic play that has been written of late; for, I thank Heaven, I am not yet so vain. But this I may modestly boast of, which the author[3] of the French Berenice has done before me, in his preface to that play, that it never failed to draw tears from the eyes of the auditors; I mean, those whose hearts were capable of so noble a pleasure: for it was not my business to take such as only come to a playhouse to see farce-fools, and laugh at their own deformed pictures. Though a certain writer that shall be nameless[4] (but you shall guess at him by what follows), being asked his opinion of this play, very gravely cocked, and cried, "I'gad, he knew not a line in it he would be author of."[5] But he is a fine facetious witty person, as my friend Sir Formal has it; and to be even with him, I know a comedy of his, that has not so much as a quibble in it that I would be author of. And so, Reader, I bid him and thee Farewell.

FOOTNOTES:

[1] James, Duke of York, afterwards James II.

[2] Rochester, whose motive in patronising Otway at this time was solely a desire to mortify Dryden.

[3] *Racine.*

[4] *Dryden.*

[5] *It will be remembered that I'gad is an expression frequently used by Bayes in the Rehearsal; a character written in ridicule of Davenant, Dryden, the Howards, &c, by the Duke of Buckingham (Dryden's Zimri), Butler, and others.*

PROLOGUE

When first our author took this play in hand,
He doubted much, and long was at a stand.
He knew the fame and memory of kings
Were to be treated of as sacred things,
Not as they're represented in this age,
Where they appear the lumber of the stage;
Used only just for reconciling tools,
Or what is worse, made villains all, or fools.
Besides, the characters he shows to-night,
He found were very difficult to write:
He found the fame of France and Spain at stake,
Therefore long paused, and feared which part to take;
Till this his judgment safest understood,
To make them both heroic as he could.
But now the greatest stop was yet unpassed;
He found himself, alas! confined too fast.
He is a man of pleasure, sirs, like you,
And therefore hardly could to business bow;
Till at the last he did this conquest get,
To make his pleasure whetstone to his wit;
So sometimes for variety he writ.
But as those blockheads, who discourse by rote,
Sometimes speak sense, although they rarely know't;
So he scarce knew to what his work would grow,
But 'twas a play, because it would be so:
Yet well he knows this is a weak pretence,
For idleness is the worst want of sense.
Let him not now of carelessness be taxed,
He'll write in earnest, when he writes the next:
Meanwhile,—
Prune his superfluous branches, never spare;
Yet do it kindly, be not too severe:
He may bear better fruit another year.

DRAMATIS PERSONÆ

PHILIP II., King of Spain.
DON CARLOS, his Son.
DON JOHN of Austria.
Marquis of POSA, the Prince's Confidant.
RUY-GOMEZ.
Officer of the Guards.

QUEEN OF SPAIN.
Duchess of EBOLI, Wife of Ruy-Gomez.
HENRIETTA.
GARCIA.

SCENE—THE COURT OF SPAIN.

DON CARLOS, PRINCE OF SPAIN.

ACT THE FIRST.

SCENE I.—An Apartment in the Palace.

KING and **QUEEN, DON CARLOS**, the **MARQUIS of POSA, RUY-GOMEZ**, the **DUCHESS of EBOLI, HENRIETTA, GARCIA, ATTENDANTS**, and **GUARDS** discovered.

KING
Happy the monarch, on whose brow no cares
Add weight to the bright diadem he wears;
Like me, in all that he can wish for, blest.
Renown and love, the gentlest calms of rest,
And peace, adorn my brow, enrich my breast.
To me great nations tributary are;
Though, whilst my vast dominions spread so far,
Where most I reign, I must pay homage, here.
[To the **QUEEN**.
Approach, bright mistress of my purest vows:
Now show me him that more religion owes
To Heaven, or to its altars more devoutly bows.

DON CARLOS
So merchants, cast upon some savage coast,
Are forced to see their dearest treasures lost.
Curse! what's obedience? a false notion made
By priests, who when they found old cheats decayed,
By such new arts kept up declining trade. [Aside.
A father! Oh!

KING
Why does my Carlos shroud
His joy, and when all's sunshine wear a cloud?
My son, thus for thy glory I provide;

From this fair charmer, and our royal bride,
Shall such a noble race of heroes spring,
As may adorn the court when thou art king.

DON CARLOS
A greater glory I can never know
Than what already I enjoy in you.
The brightest ornaments of crowns and powers
I only can admire, as they are yours.

KING
Heaven! how he stands unmoved! not the least show
Of transport.

DON CARLOS
Not admire your happiness? I do
As much admire it as I reverence you.
Let me express the mighty joy I feel:
Thus, sir, I pay my duty when I kneel.

[Kneels to the **QUEEN**.

QUEEN
How hard it is his passion to confine!
I'm sure 'tis so, if I may judge by mine. [Aside.
Alas! my lord, you're too obsequious now. [To **DON CARLOS**.

DON CARLOS
Oh! might I but enjoy this pleasure still,
Here would I worship, and for ever kneel.

QUEEN
'Fore Heaven, my lord! you know not what you do.

KING
Still there appears disturbance on his brow;
And in his looks an earnestness I read,
Which from no common causes can proceed. [Aside.
I'll probe him deep. When, when, my dearest joy,
[To the **QUEEN**.
Shall I the mighty debt of love defray?
Hence to love's secret temple let's retire,
There on his altars kindle the amorous fire,
Then, phoenix-like, each in the flame expire.—
Still he is fixed.

[Looking on **DON CARLOS**]

Gomez, observe the prince.—
Yet smile on me, my charming excellence.
[To the **QUEEN**.

Virgins should only fears and blushes show;
But you must lay aside that title now.
The doctrine which I preach, by Heaven, is good:—
Oh, the impetuous sallies of my blood!

QUEEN
To what unwelcome joys I'm forced to yield?
Now fate her utmost malice has fulfilled.
Carlos, farewell; for since I must submit—

KING
Now, winged with rapture, let us fly, my sweet.
My son, all troubles from thy breast resign,
And let thy father's happiness be thine.

[Exeunt **KING** and **QUEEN**, **RUY-GOMEZ**, **DUCHESS of EBOLI**, **HENRIETTA**, **GARCIA**, and **ATTENDANTS**.

DON CARLOS
What king, what god would not his power forego,
To enjoy so much divinity below!
Didst thou behold her, Posa?

MARQUIS of POSA
Sir, I did.

DON CARLOS
And is she not a sweet one? Such a bride!
O Posa, once she was decreed for mine:
Once I had hopes of bliss. Hadst thou but seen
How blest, how proud I was if I could get
But leave to lie a prostrate at her feet!
Even with a look I could my pains beguile;
Nay, she in pity too would sometimes smile;
Till at the last my vows successful proved,
And one day, sighing, she confessed she loved.
Oh! then I found no limits to our joy,
With eyes thus languishing we looked all day;
So vigorous and strong we darted beams,
Our meeting glances kindled into flames;
Nothing we found that promised not delight:
For when rude shades deprived us of the light,
As we had gazed all day, we dreamt all night.
But, after all these labours undergone,
A cruel father thus destroys his son;
In their full height my choicest hopes beguiles,
And robs me of the fruit of all my toils.
My dearest Posa, thou wert ever kind;
Bring thy best counsel, and direct my mind.

Re-enter **RUY-GOMEZ**.

RUY-GOMEZ
Still he is here. My lord!

DON CARLOS
Your business now?

RUY-GOMEZ
I've with concern beheld your clouded brow.
Ah! though you've lost a beauty well might make
Your strictest honour and your duty shake,
Let not a father's ills[1] misguide your mind,
But be obedient, though he has proved unkind.

DON CARLOS
Hence, cynic, to dull slaves thy morals teach;
I have no leisure now to hear thee preach:
Still you'll usurp a power o'er my will.

RUY-GOMEZ
Sir, you my services interpret ill:
Nor need it be so soon forgot that I
Have been your guardian from your infancy.
When to my charge committed, I alone
Instructed you how to expect a crown;
Taught you ambition, and war's noblest arts,
How to lead armies, and to conquer hearts;
Whilst, though but young,
You would with pleasure read of sieges got,
And smile to hear of bloody battles fought:
And, still, though not control, I may advise,

DON CARLOS
Alas! thy pride wears a too thin disguise:
Too well I know the falsehood of thy soul,
Which to my father rendered me so foul
That hardly as his son a smile I've known,
But always as a traitor met his frown.
My forward honour was ambition called;
Or, if my friends my early fame extolled,
You damped my father's smiles still as they sprung,
Persuading I repined he lived too long.
So all my hopes by you were frustrate made,
And, robbed of sunshine, withered in the shade.
Whilst, my good patriot! you disposed the crown
Out of my reach, to have it in your own.
But I'll prevent your policy—

RUY-GOMEZ
My lord,
This accusation is unjust and hard.

The king, your father, would not so upbraid
My age: is all my service thus repaid?
But I will hence, and let my master hear
How generously you reward my care;
Who, on my just complaint, I doubt not, will
At least redress the injuries I feel.

[Exit.

MARQUIS of POSA

Alas! my lord, you too severely urge
Your fate; his interest with the king is large.
Besides, you know he has already seen
The transports of your passion for the queen.
The use he may of that advantage make
You ought at least to avoid, but for her sake.

DON CARLOS

Ah! my dear friend, thou'st touched my tenderest part;
I never yet learned the dissembling art.
Go, call him back; tell him that I implore
His pardon, and will ne'er offend him more.
The queen! kind Heaven, make her thy nearest care!
Oh! fly, o'ertake him ere he goes too far.

[Exit **MARQUIS of POSA**.

How are we bandied up and down by fate!
By so much more unhappy as we're great.
A prince, and heir to Spain's great monarch born,
I'm forced to court a slave whom most I scorn;
Who like a bramble 'mongst a cedar's boughs,
Vexes his peace under whose shades he grows.
Now he returns: assist me falsehood—down,
Thou rebel passion—

Re-enter **RUY-GOMEZ** and the **MARQUIS of POSA**.

Sir, I fear I've done

[To **RUY-GOMEZ**.

You wrong; but, if I have, you can forgive.
Heaven! can I do this abject thing, and live? [Aside.

RUY-GOMEZ

Ah, my good lord, it makes too large amends,
When to his vassal thus a prince descends;
Though it was something rigid and unkind,
To upbraid your faithful servant and your friend.

DON CARLOS

Alas! no more; all jealousies shall cease;
Between us two let there be henceforth peace.
So may just Heaven assist me when I sue,
As I to Gomez always will be true.

RUY-GOMEZ

Stay, sir, and for this mighty favour take
All the return sincerity can make.
Blest in your father's love, as I'm in yours,
May not one fear disturb your happy hours!
Crowned with success may all your wishes be,
And you ne'er find worse enemies than me!

[Exeunt **DON CARLOS** and **MARQUIS of POSA**.

Nor, spite of all his greatness, shall he need:
Of too long date his ruin is decreed.
Spain's early hopes of him have been my fears;
'Twas I the charge had of his tender years,
And read in all the progress of his growth,
An untamed, haughty, hot, and furious youth;
A will unruly, and a spirit wild;
At all my precepts still with scorn he smiled.
Or when, by the power I from his father had,
Any restraint was on his pleasures laid,
Ushered with frowns on me his soul would rise,
And threaten future vengeance from his eyes.
But now to all my fears I bid adieu;
For, prince, I'll humble both your fate and you.
Here comes the star by whom my course I steer.

Re-enter **DUCHESS of EBOLI**.

Welcome, my love!

DUCHESS of EBOLI

My lord, why stay you here,
Losing the pleasures of this happy night?
When all the court are melting in delight,
You toil with the dull business of the state.

RUY-GOMEZ

Only, my fair one, how to make thee great.
Thou takest up all the business of my heart,
And only to it pleasure canst impart.
Say, say, my goddess, when shall I be blest?
It is an age since I was happy last.

DUCHESS of EBOLI

My lord, I come not hither now to hear

Your love, but offer something to your ear.
If you have well observed, you must have seen,
To-day, some strange disorders in the queen.

RUY-GOMEZ
Yes, such as youthful brides do still express,
Impatient longings for the happiness.
Approaching joys will so disturb the soul,
As needles always tremble near the pole.

DUCHESS of EBOLI
Come, come, my lord, seem not so blind; too well
I've seen the wrongs which you from Carlos feel;
And know your judgment is too good to lose
Advantage, where you may so safely choose.
Say now, if I inform you how you may
With full revenge all your past wrongs repay—

RUY-GOMEZ
Blest oracle! speak how it may be done:
My will, my life, my hopes, are all thy own.

DUCHESS of EBOLI
Hence then, and with your strictest cunning try
What of the queen and prince you can descry;
Watch every look, each quick and subtle glance;
Then we'll from all produce such circumstance
As shall the king's new jealousy advance.
Nay, sir, I'll try what mighty love you show:
If you will make me great, begin it now.
How, sir, d'ye stand considering what to do?

RUY-GOMEZ
No, but methinks I view from hence a king,
A queen, and prince, three goodly flowers spring:
Whilst on them like a subtle bee I'll prey,
Till, so their strength and virtue drawn away,
Unable to recover, each shall droop,
Grow pale, and fading hang his withered top:
Then, fraught with thyme, triumphant back I'll come,
And unlade all the precious sweets at home.

[Exit.

DUCHESS of EBOLI
In thy fond policy, blind fool, go on,
And make what haste thou canst to be undone,
Whilst I have nobler business of my own.
Was I bred up in greatness; have I been
Nurtured with glorious hopes to be a queen;
Made love my study, and with practised charms

Prepared myself to meet a monarch's arms;
At last to be condemned to the embrace
Of one whom nature made to her disgrace,
An old, imperfect, feeble dotard, who
Can only tell (alas!) what he would do?
On him to throw away my youth and bloom,
As jewels that are lost to enrich a tomb?
No, though all hopes are in a husband dead,
Another path to happiness I'll tread;
Elsewhere find joys which I'm in him denied:
Yet, while he can, let the slave serve my pride.
Still I'll in pleasure live, in glory shine;
The gallant, youthful Austria shall be mine:
To him with all my force of charms I'll move:
Let others toil for greatness, whilst I love.

[Exit.

FOOTNOTES:

[1] i.e. Faults.

ACT THE SECOND.

SCENE I.—An Orange Grove, Near the Palace.

Enter **DON JOHN of AUSTRIA.**

DON JOHN of AUSTRIA
Why should dull law rule nature, who first made
That law by which herself is now betrayed?
Ere man's corruptions made him wretched, he
Was born most noble that was born most free:
Each of himself was lord, and, unconfined,
Obeyed the dictates of his god-like mind.
Law was an innovation brought in since,
When fools began to love obedience,
And called their slavery safety and defence.
My glorious father got me in his heat,
When all he did was eminently great:
When warlike Belgia felt his conquering power,
And the proud Germans owned him emperor,
Why should it be a stain then on my blood,
Because I came not in the common road,
But born obscure, and so more like a god?
No; though his diadem another wear,
At least to all his pleasures I'll be heir.
Here I should meet my Eboli, my fair.

Enter **DUCHESS of EBOLI**.

She comes; as the bright Cyprian goddess moves,
When loose, and in her chariot drawn by doves,
She rides to meet the warlike god she loves.

DUCHESS of EBOLI
Alas! my lord, you know not with what fear
And hazard I am come to meet you here.

DON JOHN of AUSTRIA
Oh, banish it: lovers like us should fly,
And, mounted by their wishes, soar on high,
Where softest ecstasies and transports are,
While fear alone disturbs the lower air.

DUCHESS of EBOLI
But who is safe when eyes are everywhere?
Or, if we could with happiest secrecy
Enjoy these sweets, oh, whither shall we fly
To escape that sight whence we can nothing hide?

DON JOHN of AUSTRIA
Alas! lay this religion now aside;
I'll show thee one more pleasant, that which Jove
Set forth to the old world, when from above
He came himself, and taught his mortals love.

DUCHESS of EBOLI
Will nothing then quench your unruly flame?
My lord, you might consider who I am.

DON JOHN of AUSTRIA
I know you're her I love, what should I more
Regard?

DUCHESS of EBOLI [Aside.]
By Heaven, he's brave!—
But can so poor
A thought possess your breast, to think that I
Will brand my name with lust and infamy?

DON JOHN of AUSTRIA
Those who are noblest born should higher prize
Love's sweets. Oh! let me fly into those eyes!
There's something in them leads my soul astray:
As he who in a necromancer's glass
Beholds his wished-for fortune by him pass,
Yet still with greedy eyes
Pursues the vision as it glides away.

DUCHESS of EBOLI
Protect me, Heaven! I dare no longer stay;
Your looks speak danger; I feel something too
That bids me fly, yet will not let me go. [Half aside.

DON JOHN of AUSTRIA
Take vows and prayers if ever I prove false.
See at your feet the humble Austria falls.

[Kneels.

DUCHESS of EBOLI
Rise, rise.

[**DON JOHN of AUSTRIA** rises.]

My lord, why would you thus deceive? [Sighs.

DON JOHN of AUSTRIA
How many ways to wound me you contrive!
Speak, wouldst thou have an empire at thy feet?
Say, wouldst thou rule the world? I'll conquer it.

DUCHESS of EBOLI
No; above empire far I could prize you,
If you would be but—

DON JOHN of AUSTRIA
What?

DUCHESS of EBOLI
For ever true.

DON JOHN of AUSTRIA
That thou mayst ne'er have cause to fear those harms,
I'll be confined for ever in thy arms:
Nay, I'll not one short minute from thee stray;
Myself I'll on thy tender bosom lay,
Till in its warmths I'm melted all away.

Enter **GARCIA**.

GARCIA
Madam, your lord—

DUCHESS of EBOLI
Oh! fly, or I'm undone.

[Exit **GARCIA**.

DON JOHN of AUSTRIA
Must I without thy blessing then be gone?

[Kisses her hand.

DUCHESS of EBOLI
Think you that this discretion merits one?

[Pulls it back.

DON JOHN of AUSTRIA
I'm awed:
As a sick wretch, that on his death-bed lies,
Loth with his friends to part, just as he dies,
Thus sends his soul in wishes from his eyes.

[Exit.

DUCHESS of EBOLI
O Heaven! what charms in youth and vigour are!
Yet he in conquest is not gone too far;
Too easily I'll not myself resign:
Ere I am his, I'll make him surely mine;
Draw him by subtle baits into the trap,
Till he's too far got in to make escape;
About him swiftly the soft snare I'll cast,
And when I have him there, I'll hold him fast.

Enter **RUY-GOMEZ**.

RUY-GOMEZ
Thus unaccompanied I subtly range
The solitary paths of dark revenge:
The fearful deer in herds to coverts run,
While beasts of prey affect to roam alone.

DUCHESS of EBOLI
Ah! my dear lord, how do you spend your hours?
You little think what my poor heart endures;
Whilst, with your absence tortured, I in vain
Pant after joys I ne'er can hope to gain.

RUY-GOMEZ
You cannot my unkindness sure upbraid;
You should forgive those faults yourself have made.
Remember you the task you gave?

DUCHESS of EBOLI
'Tis true;
Your pardon, for I do remember now. [Sighs.
If I forgot, 'twas love had all my mind;

And 'tis no sin, I hope, to be too kind.

RUY-GOMEZ
How happy am I in a faithful wife!
O thou most precious blessing of my life!

DUCHESS of EBOLI
Does then success attend upon your toil?
I long to see you revel in the spoil.

RUY-GOMEZ
What strictest diligence could do, I've done,
To incense an angry father 'gainst his son.
I to advantage told him all that's past,
Described with art each amorous glance they cast:
So that this night he shunned the marriage-bed,
Which through the court has various murmurs spread.

Enter the **KING**, attended by the **MARQUIS of POSA**.

See where he comes with fury in his eyes:
Kind Heaven, but grant the storm may higher rise!
If't grow too loud, I'll lurk in some dark cell,
And laugh to hear my magic work so well.

KING
What's all my glory, all my pomp? how poor
Is fading greatness! or how vain is power!
Where all the mighty conquests I have seen?
I, who o'er nations have victorious been,
Now cannot quell one little foe within.
Cursed jealousy, that poisons all love's sweets!
How heavy on my heart the invader sits!
O Gomez, thou hast given my mortal wound.

RUY-GOMEZ
What is't does so your royal thoughts confound?
A king his power unbounded ought to have,
And, ruling all, should not be passion's slave.

KING
Thou counsell'st well, but art no stranger sure
To the sad cause of what I now endure.
Know'st thou what poison thou didst lately give,
And dost not wonder to behold me live?

RUY-GOMEZ
I only did as by my duty tied,
And never studied any thing beside.

KING

I do not blame thy duty or thy care:
Quickly, what passed between them more, declare.
How greedily my soul to ruin flies!
As he who in a fever burning lies
First of his friends does for a drop implore,
Which tasted once, unable to give o'er,
Knows 'tis his bane, yet still thirsts after more.
Oh, then—

RUY-GOMEZ
I fear that you'll interpret wrong;
Tis true, they gazed, but 'twas not very long.

KING
Lie still, my heart! Not long, was't that you said?

RUY-GOMEZ
No longer than they in your presence stayed.

KING
No longer? Why, a soul in less time flies
To Heaven; and they have changed theirs at their eyes.
Hence, abject fears, begone! she's all divine!
Speak, friends, can angels in perfection sin?

RUY-GOMEZ
Angels, that shine above, do oft bestow
Their influence on poor mortals here below.

KING
But Carlos is my son, and always near;
Seems to move with me in my glorious sphere.
True, she may shower promiscuous blessings down
On slaves that gaze for what falls from a crown;
But when too kindly she his brightness sees,
It robs my lustre to add more to his.
But oh! I dare not think
That those eyes should at least so humble be
To stoop to him, when they had vanquished me.

MARQUIS of POSA
Sir, I am proud to think I know the prince,
That he of virtue has too great a sense
To cherish but a thought beyond the bound
Of strictest duty. He to me has owned
How much was to his former passion due,
Yet still confessed he above all prized you.

RUY-GOMEZ
You better reconcile, sir, than advise:
Be not more charitable than you're wise.

The king is sick, and we should give him ease,
But first find out the depth of his disease.
Too sudden cures have oft pernicious grown;
We must not heal up festered wounds too soon.

KING
By this then you a power would o'er me gain,
Wounding to let me linger in the pain.
I'm stung, and won't the torture long endure:
Serpents that wound have blood those wounds to cure.

RUY-GOMEZ
Good Heaven forbid that I should ever dare
To question virtue in a queen so fair,
Though she her eyes cast on your glorious son!
Men oft see treasures, and yet covet none.

KING
Think not to blind me with dark ironies,
The truth disguised in obscure contraries.
No, I will trace his windings; all her dark
And subtlest paths, each little action mark,
If she prove false, as yet I fear, she dies.

Enter **QUEEN** attended, and **HENRIETTA**.

Ha! here! Oh, let me turn away my eyes,
For all around she'll her bright beams display:
Should I to gaze on the wild meteor stay,
Spite of myself I shall be led astray.

[Exeunt **KING** and **MARQUIS of POSA**.

QUEEN
How scornfully he is withdrawn!
Sure ere his love he'd let me know his power,
As Heaven oft thunders ere it sends a shower.
This Spanish gravity is very odd:
All things are by severity so awed,
That little Love dares hardly peep abroad.

HENRIETTA
Alas! what can you from old age expect,
When frail uneasy men themselves neglect?
Some little warmth perhaps may be behind,
Though such as in extinguished fires you'll find;
Where some remains of heat the ashes hold,
Which, if for more you open, straight are cold.

QUEEN
'Twas interest and safety of the state,—

Interest, that bold imposer on our fate;
That always to dark ends misguides our wills,
And with false happiness smooths o'er our ills.
It was by that unhappy France was led,
When, though by contract I should Carlos wed,
I was an offering made to Philip's bed.
Why sigh'st thou, Henrietta?

HENRIETTA
Who is't can
Know your sad fate, and yet from grief refrain?
With pleasure oft I've heard you smiling tell
Of Carlos' love.

QUEEN
And did it please you well?
In that brave prince's courtship there did meet
All that we could obliging call, or sweet.
At every point he with advantage stood;
Fierce as a lion, if provoked abroad;
Else soft as angels, charming as a god.

HENRIETTA
One so accomplished, and who loved you too,
With what resentments must he part with you!
Methinks I pity him—But oh! in vain:
He's both above my pity and my pain. [Aside.

QUEEN
What means this strange disorder?

HENRIETTA
Yonder view
That which I fear will discompose you too.

Enter **DON CARLOS** and **MARQUIS of POSA**.

QUEEN
Alas, the prince! There to my mind appears
Something that in me moves unusual fears.
Away, Henrietta—

[Offers to go.

DON CARLOS
Why would you be gone?
Is Carlos' sight ungrateful to you grown?
If 'tis, speak: in obedience I'll retire.

QUEEN
No, you may speak, but must advance no nigher.

DON CARLOS

Must I then at that awful distance sue,
As our forefathers were compelled to do,
When they petitions made at that great shrine,
Where none but the high priest might enter in?
Let me approach; I've nothing for your ear,
But what's so pure it might be offered there.

QUEEN

Too long 'tis dangerous for me here to stay:
If you must speak, proceed: what would you say?

[**DON CARLOS** kneels.

Nay, this strange ceremony pray give o'er.

DON CARLOS

Was I ne'er in this posture seen before?
Ah! can your cruel heart so soon resign
All sense of these sad sufferings of mine?
To your more just remembrance, if you can,
Recall how fate seemed kindly to ordain
That once you should be mine; which I believed:
Though now, alas! I find I was deceived.

QUEEN

Then, sir, you should your fate, not me upbraid.

DON CARLOS

I will not say you've broke the vows you made;
Only implore you would not quite forget
The wretch you've oft seen dying at your feet;
And now no other favour begs to have,
Than such kind pity as becomes your slave.
For 'midst your highest joys, without a crime,
At least you now and then may think of him.

QUEEN

If e'er you loved me, you would this forbear;
It is a language which I dare not hear.
My heart and faith become your father's right,
All other passions I must now forget.

DON CARLOS

Can then a crown and majesty dispense
Upon your heart such mighty influence,
That I must be for ever banished thence?
Had I been raised to all the heights of power,
In triumph crowned the world's great emperor,
Of all its riches, all its state possessed,

Yet you should still have governed in my breast.

QUEEN
In vain on her you obligations lay,
Who wants not will, but power to repay.

HENRIETTA
Yet had you Henrietta's heart, you would
At least strive to afford him all you could. [Aside.

DON CARLOS
Oh! say not you want power; you may with one
Kind look pay doubly all I've undergone.
And knew you but the innocence I bear,
How pure, how spotless all my wishes are,
You would not scruple to supply my want,
When all I ask you may so safely grant.

QUEEN
I know not what to grant; too well I find
That still at least I cannot be unkind.

DON CARLOS
Afford me then that little which I crave.

QUEEN
You shall not want what I may let you have.

[Gives her hand, sighing.

DON CARLOS
Like one
That sees a heap of gems before him cast,
Thence to choose any that may please him best;
From the rich treasure whilst I choice should make,
Dazzled with all, I know not where to take.
I would be rich—

QUEEN
Nay, you too far encroach;
I fear I have already given too much.

[Turns from him.

DON CARLOS
Oh, take not back again the appearing bliss:
How difficult's the path to happiness!
Whilst up the precipice we climb with pain,
One little slip throws us quite down again.
Stay, madam, though you nothing more can give
Than just enough to keep a wretch alive,

At least remember how I've loved—

QUEEN
I will.

DON CARLOS
That was so kind, that I must beg more still;
Let me love on: it is a very poor
And easy grant, yet I'll request no more.

QUEEN
Do you believe that you can love retain,
And not expect to be beloved again?

DON CARLOS
Yes, I will love, and think I'm happy too,
So long as I can find that you are so;
All my disquiets banish from my breast;
I will endeavour to do so at least.
[Sighing deeply.
Or, if I can't my miseries outwear,
They never more shall come to offend your ear.

QUEEN
Love then, brave prince, whilst I'll thy love admire;

[Gives her hand, which **DON CARLOS** during all this speech kisses eagerly.

Yet keep the flame so pure, such chaste desire,
That without spot hereafter we above
May meet, when we shall come all soul, all love.
Till when—Oh! whither am I run astray?
I grow too weak, and must no longer stay:
For should I, the soft charm so strong would grow,
I find that I shall want the power to go.

[Exeunt **QUEEN** and **HENRIETTA**.

DON CARLOS
Oh, sweet—
If such transport be in a taste so small,
How blest must he be that possesses all!
Where am I, Posa? Where's the queen?

[Standing amazed.

MARQUIS of POSA
My lord,
A while some respite to your heart afford:
The queen's retired—

DON CARLOS

Retired! And did she then
Just show me Heaven, to shut it in again?
This little ease augments my pain the more;
For now I'm more impatient than before,
And have discovered riches make me mad.

MARQUIS of POSA

But since those treasures are not to be had,
You should correct desires that drive you on
Beyond that duty which becomes a son.
No longer let the tyrant love invade;
The brave may by themselves be happy made.
You to your father now must all resign.

DON CARLOS

But ere he robbed me of her, she was mine.
To be my friend is all thou hast to do,
For half my miseries thou canst not know.
Make myself happy! Bid the damned do so;
Who in sad flames must be for ever tossed,
Yet still in view of the loved Heaven they've lost.

[Exeunt.

ACT THE THIRD.

SCENE I.—The Same.

Enter **DON JOHN of AUSTRIA**.

DON JOHN of AUSTRIA

How vainly would dull moralists impose
Limits on love, whose nature brooks no laws?
Love is a god, and like a god should be
Inconstant, with unbounded liberty,
Rove as he list—
I find it; for even now I've had a feast,
Of which a god might covet for a taste.
Methinks I yet
See with what soft devotion in her eyes
The tender lamb came to the sacrifice.
Oh, how her charms surprised me as I lay!
Like too near sweets they took my sense away;
And I even lost the power to reach at joy.
But those cross witchcrafts soon unravelled were,
And I was lulled in trances sweeter far:
As anchored vessels in calm harbours ride,
Rocked on the swellings of the floating tide.

How wretched's then the man, who though alone
He thinks he's blest, yet, as confined to one,
Is but at best a prisoner on a throne?

Enter the **KING** attended, **MARQUIS of POSA**, and **RUY-GOMEZ**.

KING
Ye mighty powers, whose substitutes we are,
On whom you've lain of earth the rule and care,
Why all our toils do you reward with ill,
And to those weighty cares add greater still?
Oh, how could I your deities enrage,
That blessed my youth, thus to afflict my age?
A queen and a son's incest! dismal thought!

DON JOHN of AUSTRIA
What is't so soon his majesty has brought
From the soft arms of his young bride? [To **RUY-GOMEZ**.

KING
Ay, true!
Is she not, Austria, young and charming too?
Dost thou not think her to a wonder fair?
Tell me!

DON JOHN of AUSTRIA
By Heaven, more bright than planets are:
Her beauty's force might even their power out-do.

KING
Nay, she's as false, and as unconstant too.
O Austria, that a form so outward bright
Should be within all dark and ugly night!
For she, to whom I'd dedicated all
My love, that dearest jewel of my soul,
Takes from its shrine the precious relic down,
To adorn a little idol of her own,—
My son! that rebel both to Heaven and me!
Oh, the distracting throes of jealousy!
But as a drowning wretch, just like to sink,
Seeing him that threw him in upon the brink,
At the third plunge lays hold upon his foe,
And tugs him down into destruction too;
So thou, from whom these miseries I've known,
Shalt bear me out again, or with me drown.

[Seizes roughly on **RUY-GOMEZ**.

RUY-GOMEZ
My loyalty will teach me how to wait
All the successes of my sovereign's fate.

What is't, great sir, you would command me?

KING
How!
What is't?—I know not what I'd have thee do:
Study revenge for me, 'tis that I want.

DON JOHN of AUSTRIA
Alas! what frenzy does your temper haunt?
Revenge! on whom?

KING
On my false queen and son.

RUY-GOMEZ
On them! good Heaven! what is't that they have done?
Oh, had my tongue been cursed, ere it had bred
This jealousy! [Half aside.

KING
Then cancel what thou'st said.
Didst thou not tell me that thou saw'st him stand
Printing soft vows and kisses on her hand,
Whilst in requital she such glances gave,
Would quicken a dead lover in his grave?

RUY-GOMEZ
I did; and what less could the queen allow
To him than you to every vassal show?
The affording him that little from love's store
Implied that she for you reserved much more.

KING
Oh, doubtless, she must have a wondrous store
Of love, that sells it at a rate so poor.
Now thou'dst rebate[1] my passion with advice;
And, when thou shouldst be active, wouldst be wise.
No, lead me where I may their incest see—
Do, or by Heaven—do, and I'll worship thee!
Oh, how my passions drive me to and fro!
Under their heavy weight I yield and bow.
But I'll re-gather yet my strength, and stand
Brandishing all my thunder in my hand.

MARQUIS of POSA
And may it be sent forth, and where it goes
Light fatally and heavy on your foes!
But let your loyal son and consort bear
No ill, since they of any guiltless are.
Here with my sword defiance I proclaim
To that bold traitor that dares wrong their fame.

DON JOHN of AUSTRIA
I too dare with my life their cause make good.

KING
Sure well their innocence you've understood,
That you so prodigal are of your blood.
Or wouldst thou speak me comfort? I would find
'Mongst all my counsellors at least one kind.
Yet any thing like that I must not hear;
For so my wrongs I should too tamely bear,
And weakly grow my own mean flatterer.
Posa, withdraw—

[Exit **MARQUIS of POSA**.]

—My lords, all this you've heard.

RUY-GOMEZ
Yes, I observed it, sir, with strict regard:
The young lord's friendship was too great to hide.

KING
Is he then so to my false son allied?
I am environed every way, and all
My fate's unhappy engines plot my fall.
Like Cæsar in the senate, thus I stand,
Whilst ruin threatened him on every hand.
From each side he had warning he must die;
Yet still he braved his fate, and so will I.
To strive for ease would but add more to pain:
As streams that beat against their banks in vain,
Retreating, swell into a flood again.
No, I'll do things the world shall quake to hear;
My just revenge so true a stamp shall bear,
As henceforth Heaven itself shall emulate,
And copy all its vengeance out by that.
All but Ruy-Gomez I must have withdrawn,
I've something to discourse with him alone.

[Exeunt **DON JOHN of AUSTRIA** and **ATTENDANTS**.

Now, Gomez, on thy truth depends thy fate;
Thou'st wrought my sense of wrong to such a height,
Within my breast it will no longer stay,
But grows each minute till it force its way.
I would not find myself at last deceived.

RUY-GOMEZ
Nor would I 'gainst your reason be believed.
Think, sir, your jealousy to be but fear

Of losing treasures which you hold so dear.
Your queen and son may yet be innocent:
I know but what they did, not what they meant.

KING
Meant! what should looks, and sighs, and pressings mean?
No, no; I need not hear it o'er again.
No repetitions—something must be done.
Now there's no ill I know that I would shun.
I'll fly, till them I've in their incest found,
Full charged with rage, and with my vengeance hot,
Like a grenado from a cannon shot,
Which lights at last upon the enemy's ground,
Then, breaking, deals destruction all around.

[Exit.

RUY-GOMEZ
So, now his jealousy is at the top,
Each little blast will serve to keep it up.
But stay; there's something I've omitted yet;—
Posa's my enemy; and true, he's great.
Alas! I'm armed 'gainst all that he can do;
For my snare's large enough to hold him too:
Yet I'll disguise that purpose for a while;
But when he with the rest is caught i' the toil,
I'll boldly out, and wanton in the spoil.

Re-enter **MARQUIS of POSA**.

MARQUIS of POSA
My lord Ruy-Gomez! and the king not here!
You, who so eminent a favourite are
In a king's eye, should ne'er be absent thence.

RUY-GOMEZ
No, sir, 'tis you that by a rising prince
Are cherished, and so tread a safer way,
Rich in that bliss the world waits to enjoy.

MARQUIS of POSA
Since what may bless the world we ought to prize,
I wish there were no public enemies;
No lurking serpents poison to dispense,
Nor wolves to prey on noble innocence;
No flatterers, that with royal goodness sport,
Those stinking weeds that overrun a court.

RUY-GOMEZ
Nay, if good wishes anything could do,
I have as earnest wishes, sir, as you:

That though perhaps our king enjoys the best
Of power, yet may he still be doubly blest.
May he—

MARQUIS of POSA
Nay, Gomez, you shall ne'er outdo me there;
Since for great Philip's good I would you were,
If possible, more honest than you are.

RUY-GOMEZ
Why, Posa; what defect can you discern?

MARQUIS of POSA
Nay, half your mysteries I'm yet to learn
Though this I'll boldly justify to all,—
That you contrive a generous prince's fall.

[**RUY-GOMEZ** smiles.

Nay, think not by your smiles and careless port
To laugh it off; I come not here to sport;
I do not, sir.

RUY-GOMEZ
Young lord, what meaning has
This heat?

MARQUIS of POSA
To let you see I know you're base.

RUY-GOMEZ
Nay, then, I pardon ask that I did smile:
By Heaven, I thought you'd jested all this while.
Base!

MARQUIS of POSA
Yes, more base than impotent or old.
All virtue in thee, like thy blood, runs cold:
Thy rotten putrid carcass is less full
Of rancour and contagion than thy soul.
Even now before the king I saw it plain;
But duty in that presence awed me then;
Yet there I dared thy treason with my sword:
But still
Thy villany talked all; courage had not a word.
True, thou art old; yet, if thou hast a friend,
To whom thy cursèd cause thou darest commend;
'Gainst him in public I'll the innocence
Maintain of the fair queen and injured prince.

RUY-GOMEZ

Farewell, bold champion!
Learn better how your passions to disguise;
Appear less choleric, and be more wise.

[Exit.

MARQUIS of POSA
How frail is all the glory we design,
Whilst such as these have power to undermine!
Unhappy prince! who mightst have safely stood,
If thou hadst been less great, or not so good.
Why the vile monster's blood did I not shed,
And all the vengeance draw on my own head?
My honour so had had this just defence,—
That I preserved my patron and my prince.

Enter **DON CARLOS** and the **QUEEN**.

Brave Carlos—ha! he's here. O sir, take heed;
By an unlucky fate your love is led.
The king—the king your father's jealous grown;
Forgetting her, his queen, or you, his son,
Calls all his vengeance up against you both.

DON CARLOS
Has then the false Ruy-Gomez broke his oath,
And, after all, my innocence betrayed?

MARQUIS of POSA
Yes, all his subtlest snares are for you laid.
The king within this minute will be here,
And you are ruined, if but seen with her.
Retire, my lord—

QUEEN
How! is he jealous grown?
I thought my virtue he had better known.
His unjust doubts have soon found out the way
To make their entry on our marriage day;
For yet he has not known with me a night.
Perhaps his tyranny is his delight;
And to such height his cruelty is grown,
He'd exercise it on his queen and son.
But since, my lord, this time we must obey
Our interest, I beg you would not stay:
Not seeing you, he may to me be just.

DON CARLOS
Should I then leave you, madam?

QUEEN

Yes, you must.

DON CARLOS
Not then when storms against your virtue rise.
No; since to lose you wretched Carlos dies,
He'll have the honour of it, in your cause.
This is the noblest thing that Fate could do;
She thus abates the rigour of her laws,
Since 'tis some pleasure but to die for you.

QUEEN
Talk not of death, for that even cowards dare,
When their base fears compel them to despair:
Hope's the far nobler passion of the mind;
Fortune's a mistress that's with caution kind;
Knows that the constant merit her alone,
They who, though she seem froward, yet court on.

DON CARLOS
To wretched minds thus still some comfort gleams,
And angels ease our griefs, though but with dreams.
I have too oft already been deceived,
And the cheat's grown too plain to be believed,
You, madam, bid me go.

[Looking earnestly at the **QUEEN**.

QUEEN
You must.

MARQUIS of POSA
You shall.
Alas! I love you, would not see you fall;
And yet may find some way to evade it all.

DON CARLOS
Thou, Posa, ever wert my truest friend;
I almost wish thou wert not now so kind.
Thou of a thing that's lost tak'st too much care;
And you, fair angel, too indulgent are. [To the **QUEEN**.
Great my despair; but still my love is higher.
Well—in obedience to you I'll retire;
Though during all the storm I will be nigh,
Where, if I see the danger grow too high,
To save you, madam, I'll come forth and die.

[Exit.

Re-enter **KING** and **RUY-GOMEZ**.

KING

Who would have guessed that this had ever been?

[Seeing the **MARQUIS of POSA** and the **QUEEN**

Distraction! where shall my revenge begin?
Why, he's the very bawd to all their sin;
And to disguise it puts on friendship's mask:
But his despatch, Ruy-Gomez, is thy task.
With him pretend some private conference,
And under that disguise seduce him hence;
Then in some place fit for the deed impart
The business, by a poniard to his heart.

RUY-GOMEZ
'Tis done—

KING
So, madam!

[Steps to the **QUEEN**.

QUEEN
By the fury in your eyes,
I understand you're come to tyrannize.
I hear you are already jealous grown,
And dare suspect my virtue with your son.

KING
O womankind! thy mysteries who can scan,
Too deep for easy, weak, believing man?
Hold, let me look: indeed you're wondrous fair;
So, on the outside, Sodom's apples were:
And yet within, when opened to the view,
Not half so dangerous or so foul as you.

QUEEN
Unhappy, wretched woman that I am!
And you unworthy of a husband's name!
Do you not blush?

KING
Yes, madam, for your shame.
Blush, too, my judgment e'er should prove so faint,
To let me choose a devil for a saint.
When first I saw and loved that tempting eye,
The fiend within the flame I did not spy;
But still ran on, and cherished my desires,
For heavenly beams mistook infernal fires;
Such raging fires as you have since thought fit
Alone my son, my son's hot youth should meet.
O vengeance, vengeance!

QUEEN
Poor ungenerous king!
How mean's the soul from which such thoughts must spring!
Was it for this I did so late submit
To let you whine and languish at my feet;
When with false oaths you did my heart beguile
And proffered all your empire for a smile?
Then, then my freedom 'twas I did resign,
Though you still swore you would preserve it mine.
And still it shall be so, for from this hour
I vow to hate, and never see you more.
Nay, frown not, Philip, for you soon shall know
I can resent and rage as well as you.

KING
By hell! her pride's as raging as her lust.
A guard there! seize the queen!

[Enter **GUARD**.

Re-enter **DON CARLOS**; he intercepts the **GUARDS**.

DON CARLOS
Hold, sir, be just.
First look on me, whom once you called your son,
A title I was always proud to own.

KING
Good Heaven! to merit this what have I done,
That he too dares before my sight appear?

DON CARLOS
Why, sir, where is the cause that I should fear?
Bold in my innocence, I come to know
The reason why you use this princess so.

KING
Sure I shall find some way to raise this siege:
He talks as if 'twere for his privilege.
Foul ravisher of all my honour, hence!
But stay! Guards, with the queen secure the prince.
Wherefore in my revenge should I be slow?
Now in my reach, I'll dash them at a blow.

Re-enter **DON JOHN of AUSTRIA**, with the **DUCHESS of EBOLI**, **HENRIETTA**, and **GARCIA**.

DON JOHN of AUSTRIA
I come, great sir, with wonder here, to see
Your rage grow up to this extremity
Against your beauteous queen, and loyal son;

What is't that they to merit chains have done?
Or is't your own wild jealousy alone?

KING
O Austria, thy vain inquiry cease,
If thou hast any value for thy peace.
My mighty wrongs so loud an accent bear,
'Twould make thee miserable but to hear.

DON CARLOS
Father,—if I may dare to call you so,
Since now I doubt if I'm your son or no,—
As you have sealed my doom, I may complain.

KING
Will then that monster dare to speak again?

DON CARLOS
Yes, dying men should not their thoughts disguise;
And, since you take such joy in cruelties,
Ere of my death the new delight begin,
Be pleased to hear how cruel you have been.
Time was that we were smiled on by our fate,
You not unjust, nor I unfortunate:
Then, then I was your son, and you were glad
To hear my early praise was talked abroad:
Then love's dear sweets you to me would display;
Told me where this rich, beauteous treasure lay,
And how to gain't instructed me the way.
I came, and saw, and loved, and blessed you for't.
But then when love had sealed her to my heart,
You violently tore her from my side:
And, 'cause my bleeding wound I could not hide,
But still some pleasure to behold her took,
You now will have my life but for a look;
Wholly forgetting all the pains I bore,
Your heart with envious jealousy boils o'er,
'Cause I can love no less, and you no more.

HENRIETTA
Alas! how can you hear his soft complaint,
And not your hardened, stubborn heart relent?
Turn, sir; survey that comely, awful man,
And to my prayers be cruel if you can.

KING
Away, deluder! who taught thee to sue?

DUCHESS of EBOLI
Loving the queen, what is't she less can do
Than lend her aid against the dreadful storm?

KING
Why, can the devil dwell too in that form?
This is their little engine by the bye,
A scout to watch and tell when danger's nigh.
Come, pretty sinner, thou'lt inform me all,
How, where, and when; nay, do not fear—you shall.

HENRIETTA
Ah, sir, unkind!

[Kneels.

KING
Now hold thy siren's tongue:
Who would have thought there was a witch so young?

DON JOHN of AUSTRIA
Can you to suing beauty stop your ears?

[Raises up **HENRIETTA** and makes his address to her.

Heaven lays its thunder by, and gladly hears,
When angels are become petitioners.

DUCHESS of EBOLI
Ha! what makes Austria so officious there?
That glance seems as it sent his heart to her.

[Aside to **GARCIA**.

DON CARLOS
A banquet then of blood since you design,
Yet you may satisfy yourself with mine.
I love the queen, I have confessed, 'tis true:
Proud too to think I love her more than you;
Though she, by Heaven, is clear;—but I indeed
Have been unjust, and do deserve to bleed.
There were no lawless thoughts that I did want,
Which love had power to ask, or beauty grant;
Though I ne'er yet found hopes to raise them on,
For she did still preserve her honour's throne,
And dash the bold aspiring devils down.
If to her cause you do not credit give,
Fondly against your happiness you'll strive;
As some lose Heaven, because they won't believe.

QUEEN
Whilst, prince, my preservation you design,
Blot not your virtue to add more to mine.
The clearness of my truth I'd not have shown

By any other light besides its own.—
No, sir, he through despair all this has said,
And owns offences which he never made.
Why should you think that I would do you wrong?
Must I needs be unchaste because I'm young?

KING
Unconstant wavering heart, why heavest thou so?
I shiver all, and know not what I do.
I who ere now have armies led to fight,
Thought war a sport, and danger a delight,
Whole winter nights stood under Heaven's wide roof,
Daring my foes, now am not beauty-proof.
Oh, turn away those basilisks, thy eyes;
The infection's fatal, and who sees them dies.

[Going away.

QUEEN
Oh, do not fly me; I have no design
Upon your life, for you may yet save mine.

[Kneels.

Or if at last I must my breath submit,
Here take it, 'tis an offering at your feet:
Will you not look on me, my dearest lord?

KING
Why? wouldst thou live?

QUEEN
Yes, if you'll say the word.

DON CARLOS
O Heaven! how coldly and unmoved he sees
A praying beauty prostrate on her knees!
Rise, madam—

[Steps to take her up.

KING
Bold encroacher, touch her not:
Into my breast her glances thick are shot.
Not true!—Stay, let me see—by Heaven, thou art—

[Looks earnestly on her.

A false vile woman—O my foolish heart!
I give thee life: but from this time refrain,
And never come into my sight again:

Be banished ever.

QUEEN
This you must not do,
At least till I've convinced you I am true.
Grant me but so much time; and, when that's done,
If you think fit, for ever I'll be gone.

KING
I've all this while been angry, but in vain:
She heats me first, then strokes me tame again.
Oh, wert thou true, how happy should I be!
Think'st thou that I have joy to part with thee?
No, all my kingdom for the bliss I'd give—
Nay, though it were not so—but to believe.
Come, for I can't avoid it, cheat me quite!

QUEEN
I would not, sir, deceive you if I might.
But if you'll take my oaths, by all above,
'Tis you, and only you, that I will love.

KING
Thus as a mariner that sails along,
With pleasure hears the enticing siren's song,
Unable quite his strong desires to bound,
Boldly leaps in, though certain to be drowned,—
Come to my bosom then, make no delay;

[Takes her in his arms.

My rage is hushed, and I have room for joy.

QUEEN
Again you'll think that I unjust will prove.

KING
No, thou art all o'er truth, and I all love.
Oh that we might for ever thus remain
In folded arms, and never part again!

QUEEN
Command me anything, and try your power.

KING
Then from this minute ne'er see Carlos more.—
Thou slave, that darest do ill with such a port,
For ever here I banish thee my court.
Within some cloister lead a private life,
That I may love and rule without this strife.
Here, Eboli, receive her to thy charge:

The treasure's precious, and the trust is large.
Whilst I, retiring hence, myself make fit
To wait for joys which are too fierce to meet.

[Exit.

DON CARLOS
My exile from his presence I can bear
With pleasure: but, no more to look on her!
Oh, 'tis a dreadful curse I cannot bear.
No, madam, all his power shall nothing do:
I'll stay and take my banishment from you.
Do you command me, see how far I'll fly.

QUEEN
Will Carlos be at last my enemy?
Consider, this submission I have shown,
More to preserve your safety than my own.
Ungratefully you needless ways devise,
To lose a life which I so dearly prize.

DON CARLOS
So now her fortune's made, and I am left
Alone, a naked wanderer to shift. [Aside.
Madam, you might have spared the cruelty;

[To the **QUEEN**.

Blessed with your sight, I was prepared to die.
But now to lose it drives me to despair,
Making me wish to die, and yet not dare.
Well, to some solitary shore I'll roam,
And never more into your presence come,
Since I already find I'm troublesome.

[Going.

QUEEN
Stay, sir, yet stay:—you shall not leave me so.

DON CARLOS
Ha!

QUEEN
I must talk with you before you go.
O Carlos, how unhappy is our state!
How foul a game was played us by our fate!
Who promised fair when we did first begin,
Till envying to see us like to win,
Straight fell to cheat, and threw the false lot in.
My vows to you I now remember all.

DON CARLOS
O madam, I can hear no more.

[Kneels.

QUEEN
You shall;—

[Kneels too.

For I can't choose but let you know that I,
If you'll resolve on't, yet will with you die.

DON CARLOS
Sure nobler gallantry was never known!
Good Heaven! this blessing is too much for one:
No, 'tis enough for me to die alone.
My father, all my foes, I now forgive.

QUEEN
Nay, sir, by all our loves I charge you live.
But to what country wheresoe'er you go,
Forget not me, for I'll remember you.

DON CARLOS
Shall I such virtue and such charms forget?
No, never!

QUEEN
Oh that we had never met,
But in our distant climates still been free!
I might have heard of you, and you of me:
So towards happiness more safely moved,
And never been thus wretched, yet have loved.
What makes you look so wildly? Why d'ye start?

DON CARLOS
A faint cold damp is thickening round my heart.

QUEEN
What shall we do?

DON CARLOS
Do anything but part;
Or stay so long till my poor soul expires
In view of all the glory it admires.

DUCHESS of EBOLI
In such a lover how might I be blest!
Oh! were I of that noble heart possessed,

How soft, how easy would I make his bands! [Aside.
But, madam, you forget the king's commands:

[To the **QUEEN**.

Longer to stay, your dangers will renew.

DON CARLOS
Ah, princess! lovers' pains you never knew;
Or what it is to part, as we must do.
Part too for ever!
After one minute never more to stand
Fixed on those eyes, or pressing this soft hand!
'Twere but enough to feed one, and not starve,
Yet that is more than I did e'er deserve;
Though fate to us is niggardly and poor,
That from eternity can't spare one hour.

QUEEN
If it were had, that hour would soon be gone,
And we should wish to draw another on.
No, rigorous necessity has made
Us both his slaves, and now will be obeyed.
Come, let us try the parting blow to bear.
Adieu!

[Looking at each other.

DON CARLOS
Farewell! I'm fixed and rooted here;
I cannot stir—

QUEEN
Shall I the way then show?
Now hold, my heart—

[Goes to the door, stops, and turns back again.

Nay, sir, why don't you go?

DON CARLOS
Why do you stay?

QUEEN
I won't—

DON CARLOS
You shall a while.

[Kneels.

With one look more my miseries beguile,
That may support my heart till you are gone!

QUEEN
O Eboli! thy help, or I'm undone.

[Takes hold on her.

Here, take it then, and with it too my life!

[Leans into her arms.

DON CARLOS
My courage with my tortures is at strife,
Since my griefs cowards are, and dare not kill,
I'll try to vanquish and out-toil the ill.
Well, madam, now I'm something hardier grown:
Since I at last perceive you must be gone,
To venture the encounter I'll be bold;

[Leads her to the door.

For certainly my heart will so long hold.
Farewell! be happy as you're fair and true.

QUEEN
And all Heaven's kindest angels wait on you!

[Exeunt **QUEEN, DUCHESS of EBOLI, HENRIETTA**, and **GARCIA**.

DON CARLOS
Thus long I've wandered in love's crooked way,
By hope's deluded meteor led astray;
For, ere I've half the dangerous desert crossed,
The glimmering light's gone out, and I am lost.

[Exit.

FOOTNOTES:

[1] *Make blunt.*

ACT THE FOURTH.

SCENE I.—The Ante-Chamber to the Queen's Apartment.

Enter **DON CARLOS** and **MARQUIS of POSA**.

DON CARLOS
The next is the apartment of the queen:
In vain I try, I must not venture in.

[Goes toward the door but returns.

Thus is it with the souls of murdered men,
Who to their bodies would again repair;
But, finding that they cannot enter there,
Mourning and groaning wander in the air.
Robbed of my love, and as unjustly thrown
From all those hopes that promised me a crown,
My heart, with the dishonours to me done,
Is poisoned, swells too mighty for my breast;
But it will break, and I shall be at rest.
No; dull despair this soul shall never load:
Though patience be the virtue of a god,
Gods never feel the ills that govern here,
Or are above the injuries we bear.
"Father" and "king"; both names bear mighty sense:
Yet sure there's something too in "son" and "prince".
I was born high, and will not fall less great;
Since triumph crowned my birth, I'll have my fate
As glorious and majestic too as that.
To Flanders, Posa, straight my letters send;
Tell them the injured Carlos is their friend;
And that to head their forces I design;
So vindicate their cause, if they dare mine.[1]

MARQUIS of POSA
To the rebels?

DON CARLOS
No, they're friends; their cause is just;
Or, when I make it mine, at least it must.
Let the common rout like beasts love to be dull,
Whilst sordidly they live at ease and full,
Senseless what honour or ambition means,
And ignorantly drag their load of chains.
I am a prince, have had a crown in view,
And cannot brook to lose the prospect now.
If thou'rt my friend, do not my will delay.

MARQUIS of POSA
I'll do't.

[Exit.

Enter **DUCHESS of EBOLI**.

DUCHESS of EBOLI
My lord.

DON CARLOS
Who calls me?

DUCHESS of EBOLI
You must stay.

DON CARLOS
What news of fresh affliction can you bear?

DUCHESS of EBOLI
Suppose it were the queen; you'd stay for her?

DON CARLOS
For her? yes, stay an age, for ever stay;
Stay even till time itself should pass away;
Fix here a statue never to remove,
An everlasting monument of love.
Though, may a thing so wretched as I am
But the least place in her remembrance claim?

DUCHESS of EBOLI
Yes, if you dare believe me, sir, you do;
We both can talk of nothing else but you:
Whilst from the theme even emulation springs,
Each striving who shall say the kindest things.

DON CARLOS
But from that charity I poorly live,
Which only pities, and can nothing give.

DUCHESS of EBOLI
Nothing! Propose what 'tis you claim, and I,
For aught you know, may be security.

DON CARLOS
No, madam, what's my due none e'er can pay;
There stands that angel, Honour, in the way,
Watching his charge with never-sleeping eyes,
And stops my entrance into paradise.

DUCHESS of EBOLI
What paradise? What pleasures can you know,
Which are not in my power to bestow?

DON CARLOS
Love, love, and all those eager, melting charms
The queen must yield when in my father's arms.
That queen, so excellently, richly fair,

Jove, could he come again a lover here,
Would court mortality to die for her.
O madam, take not pleasure to renew
Those pains, which if you felt, you would not do.

DUCHESS of EBOLI

Unkindly urged: think you no sense I have
Of what you feel? Now you may take your leave.
Something I had to say; but let it die.

DON CARLOS

Why, madam, who has injured you? Not I.

DUCHESS of EBOLI

Nay, sir, your presence I would not detain:
Alas! you do not hear that I complain.
Though, could you half of my misfortunes see,
Methinks you should incline to pity me.

DON CARLOS

I cannot guess what mournful tale you'd tell;
But I am certain you prepare me well.
Speak, madam.

DUCHESS of EBOLI

Say I loved, and with a flame
Which even melts my tender heart to name;
Loved too a man, I will not say ingrate,
Because he's far above my birth or fate;
Yet so far he at least does cruel prove,
He prosecutes a dead and hopeless love,
Starves on a barren rock, and won't be blest,
Though I invite him kindly to a feast.

DON CARLOS

What stupid animal could senseless lie,
Quickened by beams from that illustrious eye?

DUCHESS of EBOLI

Nay, to increase your wonder, you shall know
That I, alas! am forced to tell him too,
Till even I blush, as now I tell it you.

DON CARLOS

You neither shall have cause of shame or fear,
Whose secrets safe within my bosom are.

DUCHESS of EBOLI

Then farther I the riddle may explain:
Survey that face, and blame me if you can.

[Shows him his own picture.

DON CARLOS

Distraction of my eyes! what have they seen?
'Tis my own picture which I sent the queen,
When to her fame I paid devotion first,
Expecting bliss, but lost it: I am cursed,
Cursed too in thee, who from my saint darest steal
The only relic left her of my zeal,
And with the sacrilege attempt my heart.
Wert thou more charming than thou think'st thou art,
Almighty love preserves the fort for her,
And bids defiance to thy entrance there.

DUCHESS of EBOLI

Neglected! Scorned by father and by son!
What a malicious course my stars have run!
But since I meet with such unlucky fate
In love, I'll try how I can thrive in hate:
My own dull husband may assist in that.
To his revenge I'll give him fresh alarms,
And with the gray old wizard muster charms.
I have't; thanks, thanks, revenge! Prince, 'tis thy bane. [Aside.
Can you forgive me, sir? I hope you can. [Mildly.
I'll try to recompense the wrongs I've done,
And better finish what is ill begun.

DON CARLOS

Madam, you at so strange a rate proceed,
I shall begin to think you loved indeed.

DUCHESS of EBOLI

No matter: be but to my honour true,
As you shall ever find I'll be to you.
The queen's my charge, and you may, on that score,
Presume that you shall see her yet once more.
I'll lead you to those so-much worshipped charms,
And yield you to my happy rival's arms.

DON CARLOS

In what a mighty sum shall I be bound!
I did not think such virtue could be found.
Thou mistress of all best perfections, stay:
Fain I in gratitude would something say,
But am too far in debt for thanks to pay.

Enter **DON JOHN of AUSTRIA**.

DON JOHN of AUSTRIA

Where is that prince, he whose afflictions speak
So loud, as all hearts but his own might break?

DON CARLOS
My lord, what fate has left me, I am here,
Mere man, of all my comfort stripped and bare.
Once, like a vine, I flourished and was young,
Rich in my ripening hopes that spoke me strong:
But now a dry and withered stock am grown,
And all my clusters and my branches gone.

DON JOHN of AUSTRIA
Amongst those numbers which your wrongs deplore,
Than me there's none that can resent them more.
I feel a generous grudging in my breast,
To see such honour and such hopes oppressed.
The king your father is my brother, true;
But I see more that's like myself in you.
Free-born I am, and not on him depend,
Obliged to none, but whom I call my friend.
And if that title you think fit to bear,
Accept the confirmation of it here.

[Embraces him.

DON CARLOS
From you, to whom I'm by such kindness tied,
The secrets of my soul I will not hide.
This generous princess has her promise given,
I once more shall be brought in sight of Heaven;
To the fair queen my last devotion pay;
And then for Flanders I intend my way,
Where to the insulting rebels I'll give law,
To keep myself from wrongs, and them in awe.

DON JOHN of AUSTRIA
Prosperity to the design, 'tis good;
Both worthy of your honour and your blood.

DON CARLOS
My lord, your spreading glories flourish high,
Above the reach or shock of destiny:
Mine, early nipped, like buds untimely die.

Enter **OFFICER of the GUARD**.

OFFICER
My lord, I grieve to tell what you must hear;
They are unwelcome orders which I bear,
Which are, to guard you as a prisoner.

DON CARLOS
A prisoner! what new game of fate's begun?

Henceforth be ever cursed the name of son,
Since I must be a slave, because I'm one.
Duty! to whom? He's not my father: no.
Back with your orders to the tyrant go;
Tell him his fury drives too much one way;
I'm weary on't, and can no more obey.

DON JOHN of AUSTRIA
If asked by whose commands you did decline
Your orders, tell my brother 'twas by mine.

[Exit **OFFICER**.

DON CARLOS
Now, were I certain it would sink me quite,
I'd see the queen once more, though but in spite;
Though he with all his fury were in place,
I would caress and court her to his face.
Oh that I could this minute die! if so,
What he had lost he might too lately know,
Cursing himself to think what he has done:
For I was ever an obedient son;
With pleasure all his glories saw, when young,
Looked, and, with pride considering whence I sprung,
Joyfully under him and free I played,
Basked in his shine and wantoned in his shade—
But now,
Cancelling all whate'er he then conferred,
He thrusts me out among the common herd:
Nor quietly will there permit my stay,
But drives and hunts me like a beast of prey.
Affliction! O affliction! 'tis too great,
Nor have I ever learnt to suffer yet.
Though ruin at me from each side take aim,
And I stand thus encompassed round with flame,
Though the devouring fire approaches fast,
Yet will I try to plunge: if power waste,
I can at worst but sink, and burn at last.

[Exit.

DON JOHN of AUSTRIA
Go on, pursue thy fortune while 'tis hot:
I long for work where honour's to be got.
But, madam, to this prince you're wondrous kind.

DUCHESS of EBOLI
You are not less to Henriet, I find.

DON JOHN of AUSTRIA
Why, she's a beauty, tender, young, and fair.

DUCHESS of EBOLI

I thought I might in charms have equalled her.
You told me once my beauty was not less.
Is this your faith? are these your promises?

DON JOHN of AUSTRIA

You would seem jealous, but are crafty grown;
Tax me of falsehood to conceal your own.
Go, you're a woman—

DUCHESS of EBOLI

Yes, I know I am:
And by my weakness do deserve that name,
When heart and honour I to you resigned.
Would I were not a woman, or less kind!

DON JOHN of AUSTRIA

Think you your falsehood was not plainly seen,
When to your charge my brother gave the queen?
Too well I saw it; how did you dispense,
In looks, your pity to the afflicted prince!
Whilst I my duty paid the king, your time
You watched, and fixed your melting eyes on him;
Admired him—

DUCHESS of EBOLI

Yes, sir, for his constancy—
But 'twas with pain, to think you false to me,
When to another's eye you homage paid,
And my true love wronged and neglected laid;
Wronged, too, so far as nothing can restore.

DON JOHN of AUSTRIA

Nay, then, let's part, and think of love no more.
Farewell!

[Going.

DUCHESS of EBOLI

Farewell, if you're resolved to go:—
Inhuman Austria, can you leave me so?
Enough my soul is by your falsehood racked;
Add not to your inconstancy neglect.
Methinks you so far might have grateful proved,
Not to have quite forgotten that I loved.

DON JOHN of AUSTRIA

If e'er you loved, 'tis you, not I forget;
For a remove 'tis here too deeply set,
Firm-rooted, and for ever must remain.

[She turns away.

Why thus unkind?

DUCHESS of EBOLI
Why are you jealous then?

[Turns to him.

DON JOHN of AUSTRIA
Come, let it be no more! I'm hushed and still.
Will you forgive?

DUCHESS of EBOLI
How can you doubt my will?
I do.

DON JOHN of AUSTRIA
Then send me not away unblest.

DUCHESS of EBOLI
Till you return I will not think of rest.
Carlos will hither suddenly repair.
The next apartment's mine; I'll wait you there,
Farewell!

[She seems to weep.

DON JOHN of AUSTRIA
Oh, do not let me see a tear;
It quenches joy, and stifles appetite.
Like war's fierce god, upon my bliss I'd prey;
Who, from the furious toils of arms all day,
Returning home to love's fair queen at night,
Comes riotous and hot with full delight.

[Exit.

DUCHESS of EBOLI
He has reaped his joys, and now he would be free,
And to effect it puts on jealousy:
But I'm as much a libertine as he;
As fierce my will, as furious my desires;
Yet will I hold him; though enjoyment tires,
Though love and appetite be at the best,
He'll serve, as common meats fill up a feast,
And look like plenty, though we never taste.

Enter **RUY-GOMEZ**.

Old lord, I bring thee news will make thee young.

RUY-GOMEZ
Speak; there was always music in thy tongue.

DUCHESS of EBOLI
Thy foes are tottering, and the day's thy own;
Give them but one lift now, and they go down.
Quickly to the king, and all his doubts renew;
Appear disturbed, as if you something knew
Too difficult and dangerous to relate,
Then bring him hither labouring with the weight.
I will take care that Carlos shall be here:
So for his jealous eyes a sight prepare,
Shall prove more fatal than Medusa's head,
And he more monster seem than she e'er made.

[Exit.

Enter **KING**, attended.

KING
Still how this tyrant doubt torments my breast!
When shall I get the usurper dispossessed?
My thoughts, like birds when frighted from their rest,
Around the place where all was hushed before,
Flutter, and hardly settle any more—

[Sees **RUY-GOMEZ**.

Ha, Gomez! what art thou thus musing on?

RUY-GOMEZ
I'm thinking what it is to have a son;
What mighty cares and what tempestuous strife
Attend on an unhappy father's life;
How children blessings seem, but torments are;
When young, our folly; and when old, our fear.

KING
Why dost thou bring these odd reflections here?
Thou enviest sure the quiet which I bear.

RUY-GOMEZ
No, sir, I joy in the ease which you possess,
And wish you never may have cause for less.

KING
Have cause for less! Come nearer; thou art sad,
And look'st as thou wouldst tell me that I had.
Now, now, I feel it rising up again—

Speak quickly, where is Carlos? where the queen?
What, not a word? have my wrongs struck thee dumb?
Or art thou swollen and labouring with my doom,
Yet darest not let the fatal secret come?

RUY-GOMEZ
Heaven great infirmities to age allots:
I'm old, and have a thousand doting thoughts.
Seek not to know them, sir.

KING
By Heaven! I must.

RUY-GOMEZ
Nay, I would not be by compulsion just.

KING
Yet, if without it you refuse, you shall.

RUY-GOMEZ
Grant me then one request, I'll tell you all.

KING
Name thy petition, and conclude it done.

RUY-GOMEZ
It is, that you would here forgive your son
For all his past offences to this hour.

KING
Thou'st almost asked a thing beyond my power;
But so much goodness in the request I find,
Spite of myself, I'll for thy sake be kind.
His pardon's sealed; the secret now declare.

RUY-GOMEZ
Alas! 'tis only that I saw him here.

KING
Where? with the queen! Yes, yes, 'tis so, I'm sure;
Never were wrongs so great as I endure;
So great that they are grown beyond complaint,
For half my patience might have made a saint.
O woman! monstrous woman!
Did I for this into my breast receive
The promising, repenting fugitive?
But, Gomez, I will throw her back again;
And thou shalt see me smile and tear her then.
I'll crush her heart, where all the poison lies,
Till, when the venom's out, the viper dies,

RUY-GOMEZ
They the best method of revenge pursue
Who so contrive that it may justice show;
Stay till their wrongs appear at such a head
That innocence may have no room to plead.
Your fury, sir, at least awhile delay;
I guess the prince may come again this way:
Here I'll withdraw, and watch his privacy.

KING
And when he's fixed, be sure bring word to me;
Till then I'll bridle vengeance, and retire,
Within my breast suppress this angry fire,
Till to my eyes my wrongs themselves display;
Then, like a falcon, gently cut my way,
And with my pounces seize the unwary prey.

[Exit.

Re-enter **DUCHESS of EBOLI**.

DUCHESS of EBOLI
I've overheard the business with delight,
And find revenge will have a feast to-night.
Though thy declining years are in their wane,
I can perceive there's youth still in thy brain.
Away! the queen is coming hither.

[Exit **RUY-GOMEZ**.

Enter **QUEEN** with **ATTENDANTS**, and **HENRIETTA**.

QUEEN
Now
To all felicity a long adieu.
Where are you, Eboli?

DUCHESS of EBOLI
Madam, I'm here.

QUEEN
Oh, how fresh fears assault me everywhere!
I hear that Carlos is a prisoner made.

DUCHESS of EBOLI
No, madam, he the orders disobeyed;
And boldly owns for Flanders he intends,
To head the rebels, whom he styles his friends:
But, ere he goes, by me does humbly sue
That he may take his last farewell of you.

QUEEN
Will he then force his destiny at last?
Hence quickly to him, Eboli, make haste:
Tell him, I beg his purpose he'd delay,
Or, if that can't his resolution stay,
Say I have sworn not to survive the hour
In which I hear that he has left this shore.
Tell him, I've gained his pardon of the king;
Tell him—to stay him—tell him anything—

DUCHESS of EBOLI
One word from you his duty would restore;
And, though you promised ne'er to see him more,
Methinks you might upon so just a score.
But see, he's here.

Re-enter **DON CARLOS**.

DON CARLOS
Run out of breath by fate,
And persecuted by a father's hate,
Wearied with all, I panting hither fly,
To lay myself down at your feet, and die.

[Kneels, and kisses the **QUEEN'S** hands.

QUEEN
O too unhappy Carlos! yet unkind!
'Gainst you what harms have ever I designed,
That you should with such violence decree
Ungratefully at last to murder me?

DON CARLOS
Pour all thy curses, Heaven, upon this head,
For I've the worst of vengeance merited,
That yet I impudently live to hear
Myself upbraided of a wrong to her!

[Rises.

Say, has your honour been by me betrayed?
Or have I snares to entrap your virtue laid?
Tell me; if not, why do you then upbraid?

QUEEN
You will not know the afflictions which you give;
Was't not my last request that you would live?
I by our vows conjured it; but I see,
Forgetting them, unmindful too of me,
Regardless, your own ruin you design,
Though you are sure to purchase it with mine.

DON CARLOS

I, as you bade me live, obeyed with pride,
Though it was harder far than to have died.
But loss of liberty my life disdains;
These limbs were never made to suffer chains.
My father should have singled out some crown,
And bidden me go conquer it for my own:
He should have seen what Carlos would have done.
But to prescribe my freedom, sink me low
To base confinement, where no comforts flow,
But black despair, that foul tormentor, lies,
With all my present load of miseries,
Was to my soul too violent a smart,
And roused the sleeping lion in my heart.

QUEEN

Yet then be kind; your angry father's rage
I know the least submission will assuage;
You're hot with youth, he's choleric with age.
To him, and put a true obedience on;
Be humble, and express yourself a son.
Carlos, I beg it of you: will you not?

DON CARLOS

Methinks 'tis very hard, but yet I'll do't.
I must obey whatever you prefer,
Knowing you're all divine, and cannot err.
For, if my doom's unalterable, I shall
This way at least with less dishonour fall;
And princes less my tameness thus condemn,
When I for you shall suffer, though by him.

QUEEN

In my apartment farther we'll debate
Of this, and for a happy issue wait.
Your presence there he cannot disapprove,
When it shall speak your duty, and my love.

[Exeunt **DON CARLOS**, **QUEEN**, **HENRIETTA**, and **ATTENDANTS**.

Re-enter **RUY-GOMEZ**.

DUCHESS of EBOLI

Now, Gomez, triumph! All is ripe; the toil
Has caught them, and fate saw it with a smile.
Thus far the work of destiny was mine;
But I'm content the masterpiece be thine.
Away to the king, prepare his soul for blood,—
A mystery thou well hast understood.
Whilst I go rest within a lover's arms, [Aside.

And to my Austria lay out all my charms.

[Exit.

RUY-GOMEZ
Fate, open now thy book, and set them down:
I have already marked them for thy own.

Re-enter **KING**, and **MARQUIS of POSA** at a distance.

My lord the king?

KING
Gomez?

RUY-GOMEZ
The same.

KING
Hast seen
The prince?

RUY-GOMEZ
I have.

KING
Where is he?

RUY-GOMEZ
With the queen.

KING
Now ye that dwell in everlasting flame,
And keep records of all ye mean to damn,
Show me, if 'mongst your precedents there e'er
Was seen a son like him, or wife like her.
Hark, Gomez! didst not hear the infernals groan?
Hush, hell, a little, and they are thy own!

MARQUIS of POSA
Who should these be? the king and Gomez, sure:
Methinks I wish that Carlos were secure;
For Flanders his despatches I've prepared.

KING
Who's there? 'Tis Posa, pander to their lust.

[Drawing near to **MARQUIS of POSA**.

Now, Gomez, to his heart thy dagger thrust;
In the pursuit of vengeance drive it far;

Strike deep, and, if thou canst, wound Carlos there.

RUY-GOMEZ
I'll do't as close as happy lovers kiss:
May he strike mine, if of his heart I miss!
Thus, sir!

[Stabs **MARQUIS of POSA**.

MARQUIS of POSA
Ha, Gomez! villain! thou hast done
Thy worst: but yet I would not die alone:
Here, dog!

[Stabs at him.

RUY-GOMEZ
So brisk! then take it once again.

[As they are struggling, the despatches fall
out of **MARQUIS of POSA'S** bosom.

'Twas only, sir, to put you out of pain.

[Stabs him again, and **MARQUIS of POSA** falls.

MARQUIS of POSA
My lord the king—but life too far is gone—
I faint—be mindful of your queen and son.

[Dies.

KING
The slave in death repents, and warns me. Yes,
I shall be very mindful. What are these?

[Takes up the despatches.

For Flanders! with the prince's signet sealed!
Here's villany has yet been unrevealed.
See, Gomez, practices against my crown;

[Shows them him.

Treason and lust have joined to pull me down.
Yet still I stand like a firm sturdy rock,
Whilst they but split themselves with their own shock.
But I too long delay: give word I come.

RUY-GOMEZ
What, ho! within! The king is nigh; make room.

[**RUY-GOMEZ** draws a curtain, and discovers **DON JOHN of AUSTRIA** and the **DUCHESS of EBOLI** embracing.

KING
Now let me, if I can, to fury add,
That when I thunder I may strike them dead.

[Looking earnestly on them.

Ha! Gomez! on this truth depends thy life.
Why, that's our brother Austria!

RUY-GOMEZ
And my wife!
Embracing close. Whilst I was busy grown
In others' ruins, here I've met my own.
Oh! had I perished ere 'twas understood!

KING
This is the nest where lust and falsehood brood.
Is it not admirable?

[Exeunt **DON JOHN of AUSTRIA** and the **DUCHESS of EBOLI** embracing.

RUY-GOMEZ
Oh, sir, yes!
Ten thousand devils tear the sorceress!

KING
But they are gone, and my dishonour's near.

Re-enter **DON CARLOS** and **QUEEN**, discoursing; **HENRIETTA** and **ATTENDANTS**.

Look, my incestuous son and wife appear.
See, Gomez, how she languishes and dies.
'Sdeath! there are very pulses in her eyes.

[**DON CARLOS** approaches the **KING**.

DON CARLOS
In peace, Heaven ever guard the king from harms;
In war, success and triumph crown his arms;
Till all the nations of the world shall be
Humble and prostrate at his feet, like me!

[Kneels.

I hear your fury has my death designed;
Though I've deserved the worst, you may be kind:
Behold me as your poor unhappy son,

And do not spill that blood which is your own!

KING
Yes, when my blood grows tainted, I ne'er doubt
But for my health 'tis good to let it out:
But thine's a stranger, like thy soul, to me;
Or else be cursed thy mother's memory,
And doubly cursed be that unhappy night
In which I purchased torment with delight!

DON CARLOS
Thus then I lay aside all rights of blood.

[Rises boldly.

My mother cursed! She was all just and good,
Tyrant! too good to stay with thee below,
And therefore's blest, and reigns above thee now.
Submission! which way got it entrance here?

KING
Perhaps it came ere treason was aware.
Thy traitorous design's now come to light,
Too great and horrid to be hid in night.
See here my honour, and thy duty's stains!

[Shows the despatches.

I've paid your secretary for his pains;
He waits you there: to council with him go;

[Shows **MARQUIS of POSA'S** body.

Ask what intelligence from Flanders now.

DON CARLOS
My friend here slain, my faithful Posa 'tis.
Good Heaven! what have I done to merit this?
What temples sacked, what desolations made,
To pull down such a vengeance on my head?
This, villain, was thy work: what friend of thine [To **RUY-GOMEZ.**
Did I e'er wrong, that thou shouldst murder mine?
But I'll take care it shall not want reward—

[Draws.

KING
Courage, my Gomez, since thy king's thy guard.
Come, rebel, and thy villanies fulfil!

DON CARLOS

No; though unjust, you are my father still;

[Throws away his sword.

And from that title must your safety own:
'Tis that which awes my hand, and not your crown.
'Tis true, all there contained I had designed:
To such a height your jealousy was grown,
It was the only way that I could find
To work your peace, and to procure my own.

KING
Thinking my youth and vigour to decrease,
You'd ease me of my crown to give me peace.

DON CARLOS
Alas! you fetch your misconstructions far:
The injuries to me, and wrongs to her,
Were much too great for empire to repair.
When you forgot a father's love, and quite
Deprived me of a son's and prince's right,
Branded my honour, and pursued my life,
My duty long with nature was at strife.
Not that I feared my memory or name
Could suffer by the voice of common fame;
A thing I still esteemed beneath my pride:
For, though condemned by all the world beside,
Had you but thought me just, I could have died.
At last this only way I found, to fly
Your anger, and divert your jealousy:—
To go to Flanders, and be so removed
From all I ever honoured, ever loved;
There in your right hoping I might complete,
Spite of my wrongs, some action truly great;
Thus by my faith and sufferings to out-wear
Your hate, and shun that storm which threatened here.

QUEEN
And can this merit hate? He would forego
The joys and charms of courts to purchase you;
Banish himself, and stem the dangerous tide
Of lawless outrage and rebellious pride.

KING
How evenly she pleads in his defence!
So blind is guilt when 'twould seem innocence.
She thinks her softness may my rage disarm.
No, sorceress, you're mistaken in your charm,
And, whilst you soothe, do but assist the storm!
Do, take full view of your tall able slave;

[**QUEEN** looks on **DON CARLOS**.

Look hard; it is the last you're like to have.

DON CARLOS
My life or death are in your power to give.

KING
Yes, and thou diest.

DON CARLOS
Not till she give me leave:
She is the star that rules my destiny;
And, whilst her aspect's kind, I cannot die.

QUEEN
No, prince, for ever live, be ever blest.

KING
Yes, I will send him to his eternal rest.
Oh! had I took the journey long ago,
I ne'er had known the pains that rack me now.

QUEEN
What pains? what racks?

[Approaching.

KING
Avoid, and touch me not!
I see thee foul, all one incestuous blot;
Thy broken vows are in thy guilty face.

QUEEN
Have I then in your pity left no place?

KING
Oh! thus it was you drew me in before,
With promises you ne'er would see him more.
But now your subtlest wiles too weak are grown;
I've gotten freedom, and I'll keep my own.

QUEEN
May you be ever free! But can your mind
Conceive that any ill was here designed?
He hither came, only that he might show
Obedience, and be reconciled to you.
You saw his humble, dutiful address.

KING
But you beforehand signed the happy peace.

Re-enter **DUCHESS of EBOLI**.

O princess, thank you for the care you take.
Tell me, how got this monster entrance? speak.

DUCHESS of EBOLI
Heaven witness 'twas without my knowledge done.

RUY-GOMEZ
No, she had other business of her own. [Aside.

O blood and murder!

KING
All are false: a guard!

Enter **GUARD**.

Seize on that traitor!

[Pointing to **DON CARLOS**.

DON CARLOS
Welcome; I'm prepared.

QUEEN
Stay, sir, let me die too: I can obey.

KING
No, thou shalt live. [Seemingly kind.]
By Heaven, but not a day! [Aside.
I a revenge so exquisite have framed,
She unrepenting dies, and so she's damned.

HENRIETTA
If ever pity could your heart engage,
If e'er you hope for blessings on your age,
Incline your ears to a poor virgin's prayer!

KING
I dare not venture thee, thou art too fair.
What wouldst thou say?

HENRIETTA
Destroy not in one man
More virtue than the world can boast again.
View him the eldest pledge of your first love,
Your virgin joys; that may some pity move—

KING

No; for the wrongs I suffer weigh it down:
I'd now not spare his life to save my own.
Away! by thy soft tongue I'll not be caught.

HENRIETTA
By all that hopes can frame I beg: if not,
May you by some base hand unpitied die,
And childless mothers curse your memory!
By honour, love, by life—

KING
Fond girl, away:
By Heaven, I'll kill thee else! Still darest thou stay?
Cannot death terrify thee?

HENRIETTA
No; for I,
If you refuse me, am resolved to die.

DON CARLOS
Kind fair one, do not waste your sorrows here
On me, too wretched, and not worth a tear.
There yet for you are mighty joys in store,
When I in dust am laid, and seen no more.—
O madam!

[To the **QUEEN**.

QUEEN
O my Carlos! must you die
For me? no mercy in a father's eye?

DON CARLOS
Hide, hide your tears, into my soul they dart
A tenderness that misbecomes my heart:
For, since I must, I like a prince would fall,
And to my aid my manly spirits call.

QUEEN
You, like a man, as roughly as you will
May die, but let me be a woman still!

[Weeps.

KING
Thou'rt woman, a true copy of the first,
In whom the race of all mankind was cursed.
Your sex by beauty was to Heaven allied;
But your great lord, the devil, taught you pride.
He too an angel, till he durst rebel;
And you are, sure, the stars that with him fell.

Weep on! a stock of tears like vows you have,
And always ready when you would deceive.

QUEEN
Cruel! inhuman! O my heart! why should
I throw away a title that's so good,
On one a stranger to whate'er was so?
Alas, I'm torn, and know not what to do.
The just resentment of my wrong's so great,
My spirits sink beneath the heavy weight.
Tyrant, stand off! I hate thee, and will try
If I have scorn enough to make me die.

DON CARLOS
Blest angel, stay!

[Takes her in his arms.

QUEEN
Carlos, the sole embrace
You ever took, you have before his face.

DON CARLOS
No wealthy monarch of the plenteous East,
In all the glories of his empire dressed,
Was ever half so rich, or half so blest.
But from such bliss how wretched is the fall!
They too like us must die, and leave it all.

KING
All this before my face! what soul could bear't?
Go, force her from him!

[**OFFICER** approaches.

DON CARLOS
Slave, 'twill cost thy heart.
Thou'dst better meet a lion on his way,
And from his hungry jaws reprize the prey!
She's mistress of my soul, and to prepare
Myself for death, I must consult with her.

RUY-GOMEZ
Have pity! [Ironically.

KING
Hence! how wretchedly he rules
That's served by cowards, and advised by fools!
Oh, torture!

DON CARLOS

Rouse, my soul! consider now
That to thy blissful mansion thou must go.
But I so mighty joys have tasted here,
I hardly shall have sense of any there:
Oh, soft as blossoms, and yet sweeter far!

[Leaning on her bosom.

Sweeter than incense which to Heaven ascends,
Though 'tis presented there by angels' hands.

KING
Still in his arms! Cowards, go tear her forth!

DON CARLOS
You'll sooner from its centre shake the earth:
I'll hold her fast till my last hour is nigh;
Then I'll bequeath her to you when I die.

KING
Cut off his hold! or any thing—

DON CARLOS
Ay, come;
Here kill, and bear me hence into my tomb.
I'd have my monument erected here,
With broken mangled limbs still clasping her.

QUEEN
Hold, and I'll quit his arms—

[The Guards offer their axes. They part.

KING
Now bear him hence.

QUEEN
O horrid tyrant!

[**GUARDS** are hurrying **DON CARLOS** off.

Stay, unhappy prince—
Turn, turn! O torment! must I leave you so?
No, stay, and take me with you where you go.

DON CARLOS
Hark, slaves, my goddess summons me to stay.
Dogs! have you eyes, and can you disobey?
See her! Oh, let me but just touch my bliss.

[Pressing forward.

KING
By hell! he shan't. Slaves, are ye mine or his?

QUEEN
My life—

DON CARLOS
My soul, farewell!

[Exeunt **GUARDS** with **DON CARLOS**.

QUEEN
He's gone, he's gone!
Now, tyrant, to thy rage I'm left alone;
Give me my death, that hate both life and thee.

KING
I know thou dost; yet live.

QUEEN
O misery!

[Throws herself down.

Why was I born to be thus cursed? or why
Should life be forced, when 'tis so sweet to die?

KING [To **DUCHESS of EBOLI**]
Thou, woman, hast been false; but, to renew
Thy credit in my heart, assist me now.
Prepare a draught of poison, such as will
Act slow, and by degrees of torment kill.
Give it the queen, and, to prevent all sense
Of dying, tell her I've released the prince,
And that ere morning he'll attend her. I
In a disguise his presence will supply;
So glut my rage, and smiling see her die.

DUCHESS of EBOLI
Your majesty shall be obeyed.

RUY-GOMEZ
Do, work thy mischiefs to their last degree,
And when they're in their height I'll murder thee.

[Aside.

KING
Now, Gomez, ply my rage and keep it hot:
O'er love and nature I've the conquest got.

Still charming beauty triumphs in her eyes:

[Looking at the **QUEEN**.

Yet for my honour and my rest she dies.

[Exeunt **QUEEN** and **WOMEN**.

But, oh! what ease can I expect to get,
When I must purchase at so dear a rate?

[Exeunt.

FOOTNOTES:

[1] Don Carlos actually engaged in intrigues with the principals of the revolution which broke out in the Low Countries during the tyrannical reign of Philip II., and ended in the establishment of the Dutch republic.—Thornton.

ACT THE FIFTH.

SCENE I.—An Apartment in the Palace.

Enter **KING** disguised.

KING
'Tis night; the season when the happy take
Repose, and only wretches are awake.
Now discontented ghosts begin their rounds,
Haunt ruined buildings and unwholesome grounds;
Or at the curtains of the restless wait,
To frighten them with some sad tale of fate.
When I would rest, I can no rest obtain:
The ills I've borne even o'er my slumbers reign,
And in sad dreams torment me o'er again.
The fatal business is ere this begun:
I'm shocked, and start to think what I have done.
But I forget how I that Philip am
So much for constancy renowned by fame;
Who through the progress of my life was ne'er
By hopes transported, or depressed by fear.
No, it is gone too far to be recalled,
And steadfastness will make the act extolled.

Enter **DUCHESS of EBOLI**, in a night-gown.

Who? Eboli?

DUCHESS of EBOLI

My lord.

KING
Is the deed done?

DUCHESS of EBOLI
'Tis, and the queen to seek repose is gone.

KING
Can she expect it, who allowed me none?
No, Eboli; her dreams must be as full
Of horror, and as hellish as her soul.
Does she believe the prince has freedom gained?

DUCHESS of EBOLI
She does.

KING
How were the tidings entertained?

DUCHESS of EBOLI
O'er all her face young wandering blushes were,
Such as speak hopes too weak to conquer fear:—
But when confirmed, no lover e'er so kind;
She clasped me fast, caressed, and called me friend.
Which opportunity I took, to give
The poison; and till day she cannot live.

KING
Quickly then to her; say that Carlos here
Waits to confirm his happiness with her.
Go, that my vengeance I may finish quite:
'Twould be imperfect, should I lose the sight.
But to contrive that I may not be known,
And she may still mistake me for my son,
Remove all light but that which may suffice
To let her see me scorn her when she dies.

DUCHESS of EBOLI
You'll find her all in rueful sables clad,
With one dim lamp that yields imperfect light,
Such as in vaults assist the ghastly shade,
Where wretched widows come to weep at night.
Thus she resolves to die, or living mourn,
Till Carlos shall with liberty return.

[Exit.

KING
O steadfast sin! incorrigible lust!
Not damned! it is impossible; she must.

How do I long to see her in her pains,
The poisonous sulphur rolling through her veins!

Enter **DON JOHN of AUSTRIA** and **ATTENDANTS**.

Who's there? my brother?

DON JOHN of AUSTRIA
Yes, sir, and your friend.
What can your presence here so late intend?

KING
O Austria! Fate's at work; a deed's in hand
Will put thy youthful courage to a stand.
Survey me; do I look as heretofore?

DON JOHN of AUSTRIA
You look like King of Spain, and lord of power;
Like one who still seeks glory on the wing;
You look as I would do, were I a king.

KING
A king! why I am more, I'm all that can
Be counted miserable in a man.
But thou shalt see how calm anon I'll grow;
I'll be as happy and as gay as thou.

DON JOHN of AUSTRIA
No, sir; my happiness you cannot have,
Whilst to your abject passions thus a slave.
To know my ease, you thoughts like mine must bring,
Be something less a man, and more a king.

KING
I'm growing so. 'Tis true that long I strove
With pleading nature, combated with love,
Those witchcrafts that had bound my soul so fast;
But now the date of the enchantment's past:
Before my rage like ruins down they fall,
And I mount up true monarch o'er them all.

DON JOHN of AUSTRIA
I know your queen and son you've doomed to die,
And fear by this the fatal hour is nigh.
Why would you cut a sure succession off,
At which your friends must grieve, and foes will laugh;
As if, since age has from you took away
Increase, you'd grow malicious, and destroy?

KING
Doubt it not, Austria: thou my brother art,

And in my blood I'm certain hast a part.
Only the justice of my vengeance own,—
Thou'rt heir of Spain, and my adopted son.

DON JOHN of AUSTRIA
I must confess there in a crown are charms,
Which I would court in bloody fields and arms;
But in my nephew's wrong I must decline,
Since he must be extinguished ere I shine.
To mount a throne o'er battlements I'd climb,
Where Death should wait on me, not I on him.
Did you e'er love, or have you ever known
The mighty value of so brave a son?

KING
I guessed I should be treated thus before;
I know it is thy kindness, but no more.
Thou, living free, alas! art easy grown
And think'st all hearts as honest as thy own.

DON JOHN of AUSTRIA
Not, sir, so easy as I must be bold,
And speak what you perhaps would have untold;
That you're a slave to the vilest that obey,
Such as disgrace on royal favour lay,
And blindly follow as they lead astray:
Voracious varlets, sordid hangers-on;
Best by familiarity they're known,
Yet shrink at frowns: but when you smile they fawn.
They're these have wronged you, and abused your ears,
Possessed your mind with false misgrounded fears.

KING
Misgrounded fears? Why, is there any truth
In women's vows, or disobedient youth?
I sooner would believe this world were Heaven,
Where I have nought but toils and torment met,
And never comfort yet to man was given.
But thou shalt see how my revenge I'll treat.

[A curtain is drawn, and discovers the **QUEEN** alone in mourning on her couch, with a lamp by her.

Look where she sits, as quiet and serene   [Ironically.
As if she never had a thought of sin,
In mourning, her wronged innocence to show!
She has sworn't so oft, that she believes it true.
O'erwhelmed with sorrow she'll in darkness dwell:
So we have heard of witches in a cell,
Treating with fiends, and making leagues with hell.

[The **QUEEN** rises and comes towards him.

QUEEN

My lord! Prince Carlos! may it be believed?
Are my eyes blessed; and am I not deceived?

KING

My queen, my love, I'm here—

[Embraces her.

QUEEN

My lord the king!
This is surprising kindness which you bring.
Can you believe me innocent at last?
Methinks my griefs are half already past.

KING

O tongue, in nothing practised but deceit!
Too well she knew him, not to find the cheat. [Aside.
Yes, vile incestuous woman, it is I,
The king: look on me well, despair, and die.

QUEEN

Why had you not pronounced my doom before,
Since to affliction you could add no more?
Methinks death is less welcome, when I find
You could but counterfeit a look that's kind.

KING

No, now thou'rt fit for death: had I believed
Thou couldst have been more wicked, thou hadst lived,—
Lived and gone on in lust and riot still;
But I perceived thee early ripe for hell:
And, that of the reward thou mightst not miss,
This night thou'st drank thy bane, thou'rt poisoned; yes,
Thou art—

QUEEN

Then welcome everlasting bliss!
But, ere I die, let me here make a vow,—
By Heaven, and all I hope for there, I'm true!

KING

Vows you had always ready when you spoke:
How many of them have you made, and broke!
Yet there's a Power that does your falsehood hear,
A just one too, that lets thee live to swear.
How comes it that above such mercy dwells,
To permit sin, and make us infidels?

QUEEN

You have been ever so to all that's good,
My innocence had else been understood.
At first your love was nothing but your pride.
When I arrived to be the prince's bride,
You then a kind indulgent father were;
But, finding me unfortunately fair,
Thought me a prize too rich to be possessed
By him, and forced yourself into my breast,
Where you maintained an unresisted power;
Not your own daughter could have loved you more,
Till, conscious of your age, my faith was blamed,
And I a lewd adulteress proclaimed,
Accused of foulest incest with your son—
What more could my worst enemy have done?

KING

Nothing, I hope; I would not have it said
That in my vengeance any fault I made.
Love me! O low pretence, too feebly built!
But 'tis the constant fault of dying guilt
Even to the last to cry they're innocent,
When their despair's so great, they can't repent.

QUEEN

Thus having urged your malice to the head,
You spitefully are come to rail me dead.
Had I been man, and had an impious wife,
With speedy fury I'd have snatched her life;
Torn a broad passage open to her heart,
And there have ransacked each polluted part;
Triumphed and laughed to have seen the issuing flood,
And wantonly have bathed my hands in blood.
That had outdone the low revenge you bring,
Much fitter for a woman than a king.

KING

I'm glad I know what death you'd wish to have:
You would go down in silence to your grave;
Remove from future fame, as present times,
And bury with you, if you could, your crimes.
No, I will have my justice understood,
Proclaim thy falsehood and thy lust aloud.

QUEEN

About it then, the noble work begin;
Be proud, and boast how cruel you have been.
Oh, how a monarch's glory 'twill advance!
Do, quickly let it reach the ears of France.
I've there a royal brother that is young,
Who'll certainly revenge his sister's wrong;
Into thy Spain a mighty army bring,

Tumble thee from thy throne a wretched thing,
And make it quite forgot thou e'er wert king.

KING
I ne'er had pleasure with her till this night:
The viper finds she's crushed, and fain would bite.—
Oh! were he here, and durst maintain that word,
I'd like an eagle seize the callow bird,
And gripe him till the dastard craven cried;
Then throw him panting by his sister's side.

QUEEN
Alas! I faint and sink; my lord, your hand!

[To **DON JOHN of AUSTRIA**.

My spirits fail, and I want strength to stand.

DON JOHN of AUSTRIA
O jealousy!
A curse which none but he that bears it knows!

[Leads her to a chair.

So rich a treasure who would live to lose?

KING
The poison works, Heaven grant there were enough!
She is so foul, she may be poison-proof.
Now my false fair one—

QUEEN
Tyrant, hence, begone!
This hour's my last, and let it be my own.
Away, away! I would not leave the light
With such a hated object in my sight.

KING
No, I will stay, and even thy prayers prevent;
I would not give thee leisure to repent;
But let thy sins all in one throng combine
To plague thy soul, as thou hast tortured mine.

QUEEN
Glut then your eyes, your tyrant-fury feed,
And triumph; but remember, when I'm dead,
Hereafter on your dying pillows you
May feel those tortures which you give me now.
Go on, your worst reproaches I can bear,
And with them all you shall not force a tear.

KING
Thus, Austria, my lost freedom I obtain,
And once more shall appear myself again.
Love held me fast whilst, like a foolish boy,
I of the thing was fond because 'twas gay;
But now I've thrown the gaudy toy away.

DUCHESS of EBOLI [Within]
Help! murder! help!

KING
See, Austria, whence that cry.
Call up our guards; there may be danger nigh.

Enter **GUARDS**; then re-enter **DUCHESS of EBOLI** in her night-dress, wounded and bleeding; **RUY-GOMEZ** pursuing her.

DUCHESS of EBOLI
Oh! guard me from that cruel murderer:
But 'tis in vain, the steel has gone too far.
Turn, wretched king, I've something to unfold;
Nor can I die till the sad secret's told.

KING
The woman's mad; to some apartment by
Remove her, where she may grow tame and die.—
Fate came abroad to night, resolved to range:
I love a kind companion in revenge.

[Hugs **RUY-GOMEZ**.

DUCHESS of EBOLI
If in your heart truth any favour wins,
If e'er you would repent of secret sins,
Hear me a word.

KING
What wouldst thou say? Be brief.

DUCHESS of EBOLI
Do what you can to save that precious life;
Try every art that may her death prevent:
You are abused, and she is innocent.
When I perceived my hopes of you were vain,
Led by my lust, I practised all my charms
To gain the prince, Don Carlos, to my arms;
But, there too crossed, I did the purpose change,
And pride made him my engine for revenge;

[To **RUY-GOMEZ**.

Taught him to raise your growing jealousy.
Then my wild passion at this prince did fly,

[To **DON JOHN of AUSTRIA**.

And that was done for which I now must die.

KING
Ha! Gomez, speak, and quickly; is it so?

RUY-GOMEZ
I'm sorry you should doubt if't be or no.
She, by whose lust my honour was betrayed,
Cannot want malice now to take my head;
And therefore does this penitence pretend.

DUCHESS of EBOLI
O Austria! take away that ugly fiend:
He smiles and mocks me, waiting for my soul;
See how his glaring fiery eyeballs roll!

RUY-GOMEZ
Thus is her fancy tortured by her guilt:
But, since you'll have my blood, let it be spilt.

KING [To **RUY-GOMEZ**].
No more!—[To **DUCHESS of EBOLI**]
Speak on, I charge thee, by the rest
Thou hopest, the truth, and as thou shalt be blest.

DUCHESS of EBOLI
As what I've said is so,
There may I find, where I must answer all,
What most I need, Heaven's mercy on my soul!

[Dies.

KING
Heaven! she was sensible that she should die,
And durst not in the minute tell a lie.

DON JOHN of AUSTRIA
His guilt's too plain; see his wild staring eye.
By unconcern he would show innocence;
But hardened guilt ne'er wanted the pretence
Of great submission, when't had no defence.
Thus, whilst of life you show this little care,
You seem not guiltless, but betray despair.

KING
His life! What satisfaction can that give?

But oh! in doubt I must for ever live,
And lose my peace—yet I the truth will find;
I'll rack him for't. Go, in this minute bind
Him to the wheel—

RUY-GOMEZ
How have I this deserved,
Who only your commands obeyed and served?
What would you have me do?

KING
I'd have thee tell
The truth: do, Gomez; all shall then be well.

RUY-GOMEZ
Alas! like you, sir, in a cloud I'm lost.
And can but tell you what I think, at most.
You set me as a spy upon the prince,
And I still brought the best intelligence
I could; till, finding him too much aware
Of me, I nearer measures took by her:
Which if I after a false copy drew,
'Tis I have been unfortunate as you.

KING
And is this all thou hast for life to show?

RUY-GOMEZ
Dear sir, your pardon, it is all I know.

KING
Then villain, I am damned as well as thou.
Heaven! where is now thy sleeping providence,
That took so little care of innocence?
O Austria, had I to thy truth inclined,
Had I been half so good as thou wert kind!
But I'm too tame; secure the traitor. Oh!

[**GUARDS** seize **RUY-GOMEZ**.

Earth, open! to thy centre let me go!
And there for ever hide my impious head!
Thou fairest, purest creature Heaven e'er made,
Thy injured truth too late I've understood:
Yet live, and be immortal as thou'rt good.

QUEEN
Can you to think me innocent incline
On her bare word, and would not credit mine?
The poison's very busy at my heart;
Methinks I see Death shake his threatening dart.

Why are you kind, and make it hard to die?
Persist, continue on the injury;
Call me still vile, incestuous, all that's foul—

KING
Oh, pity, pity my despairing soul!
Sink it not quite. Raise my physicians straight;
Hasten them quickly ere it be too late;
Propose rewards may set their skill at strife:
I'll give my crown to him that saves her life.
Cursed dog! [To **RUY-GOMEZ**.

DON JOHN of AUSTRIA
Vile prostitute!

KING
Revengeful fiend!
But I've forgotten half—to Carlos send;
Prevent what his despair may make him do.

Enter **HENRIETTA**.

HENRIETTA
O horror, horror! everlasting woe!
The prince, the prince!

KING
Ha! speak.

HENRIETTA
He dies, he dies!
Within upon his couch he bleeding lies,
Just taken from a bath, his veins all cut,
From which the springing blood flows swiftly out.
He threatens death on all that shall oppose
His fate, to save that life which he will lose.

KING
Dear Austria, hasten, all thy interest use;
Tell him it is to friendship an offence,
And let him know his father's penitence.
Beg him to live.

RUY-GOMEZ
Since you've decreed my death, know 'twill be hard:
The bath by me was poisoned when prepared.
I owed him that for his late pride and scorn.

KING
There never was so cursed a villain born.
But by revenge such pains he shall go through

As even religious cruelty ne'er knew.
Rack him! I'll broil him, burn him by degrees,
Fresh torments for him every hour devise,
Till he curse Heaven, and then the caitiff dies.

QUEEN
My faithful Henrietta, art thou come
To wait thy unhappy mistress to her tomb?
I brought thee hither from thy parents young,
And now must leave thee to Heaven knows what wrong.
But Heaven to its protection will receive
Such goodness; let it then thy queen forgive!

HENRIETTA
How much I loved you, madam, none can tell;
For 'tis unspeakable, I loved so well.
A proof of it the world shall quickly find;
For, when you die, I'll scorn to stay behind.

Enter **DON CARLOS**, supported between two **ATTENDANTS** and bleeding.

DON JOHN of AUSTRIA
See, sir, your son.

KING
My son! But oh! how dare
I use that name, when this sad object's near?
See, injured prince, who 'tis thy pardon craves,
No more thy father, but the worst of slaves:
Behold the tears that from these fountains flow.

DON CARLOS
I come to take my farewell, ere I go
To that bright dwelling where there is no room
For blood, and where the cruel never come.

KING
I know there is not, therefore must despair.
O Heaven! his cruelty I cannot bear.—
Dost thou not hear thy wretched father sue?

DON CARLOS
My father! speak the words once more; is't you?
And may I think the dear conversion true?
Oh that I could!

KING
By Heaven thou must—it is!
Let me embrace and kiss thy trembling knees.
Why wilt thou die? no, live, my Carlos, live,
And all the wrongs that I have done forgive!

DON CARLOS
Life was my curse, and given me sure in spite.
Oh! had I perished when I first saw light,
I never then these miseries had brought
On you, nor by you had been guilty thought.
Prop me: apace I feel my life decay.
The little time on earth I have to stay,
Grant I without offence may here bestow;

Pointing to the **QUEEN**.

You cannot certainly be jealous now.

KING
Break, break, my heart!

[Leads **DON CARLOS** to the chair.

DON CARLOS
You've thus more kindness shown
Than if you'd crowned, and placed me on your throne.
Methinks so highly happy I appear
That I could pity you, to see you there.
Take me away again:—you are too good.

QUEEN
Carlos, is't you? Oh, stop that royal flood;
Live, and possess your father's throne, when I
In dark and gloomy shades forgotten lie.

DON CARLOS
Crowns are beneath me; I have higher pride:
Thus on you fixed, and dying by your side,
How much a life and empire I disdain!
No, we'll together mount, where both shall reign
Above all wrongs, and never more complain.

QUEEN
O matchless youth! O constancy divine!
Sure there was never love that equalled thine;
Nor any so unfortunate as mine.
Henceforth forsaken virgins shall in songs,
When they would ease their own, repeat thy wrongs;
And in remembrance of thee, for thy sake,
A solemn annual procession make;
In chaste devotion as fair pilgrims come,
With hyacinths and lilies deck thy tomb.
But one thing more, and then, vain world, adieu!
It is to reconcile my lord and you.

DON CARLOS

He has done no wrong to me; I am possessed
Of all, beyond my expectation blest.
But yet methinks there's something in my heart
Tells me, I must not too unkindly part.—
Father, draw nearer, raise me with your hand;
Before I die, what is't you would command?

KING

Why wert thou made so excellently good?
And why was it no sooner understood?
But I was cursed, and blindly led astray;
Oh! for thy father, for thy father pray.
Thou mayst ask that which I'm too vile to dare;
And leave me not tormented by despair.

DON CARLOS

Thus then with the remains of life we kneel.

[**DON CARLOS** and the **QUEEN** sink out of their chairs and kneel.

May you be ever free from all that's ill!

QUEEN

And everlasting peace upon you dwell!

KING

No more: this virtue's too divinely bright;
My darkened soul, too conversant with night,
Grows blind, and overcome with too much light.
Here, raise them up—gently—ye slaves, down, down!
Ye glorious toils, a sceptre and a crown,
For ever be forgotten; in your stead,
Only eternal darkness wrap my head.

QUEEN

Where are you? oh! farewell, I must be gone.

KING

Blest happy soul, take not thy flight so soon:
Stay till I die, then bear mine with thee too,
And guard it up, which else must sink below.

QUEEN

From all my injuries and all my fears,
From jealousy, love's bane, the worst of cares,
Thus I remove to find that stranger, rest.
Carlos, thy hand, receive me on thy breast;
Within this minute how shall we be blest!

DON CARLOS

Oh, far above
Whatever wishes framed, or hopes designed;
Thus, where we go, we shall the angels find
For ever praising, and for ever kind.

QUEEN
Make haste; in the first sphere I'll for you stay;
Thence we'll rise both to everlasting day.
Farewell—

[Dies.

DON CARLOS
I follow you; now close my eyes;

[Leans on her bosom.

Thus all o'er bliss the happy Carlos dies.

[Dies.

KING
They're gone, they're gone, where I must ne'er aspire.
Run, sally out, and set the world on fire;
Alarum Nature, let loose all the winds,
Set free those spirits whom strong magic binds;
Let the earth open all her sulphurous veins,
The fiends start from their hell, and shake their chains;
Till all things from their harmony decline,
And the confusion be as great as mine!
Here I'll lie down, and never more arise,
Howl out my life, and rend the air with cries.

DON JOHN of AUSTRIA
Hold, sir, afford your labouring heart some ease.

KING
Oh! name it not: there's no such thing as peace.
From these warm lips yet one soft kiss I'll take.
How my heart beats! why won't the rebel break?
My love, my Carlos, I'm thy father—speak.
Oh! he regards not now my miseries,
But's deaf to my complaint, as I have been to his.
Oh! now I think on't better, all is well.
Here's one that's just descending into hell;
How comes it that he's not already gone?
The sluggard's lazy, but I'll spur him on.
Hey! how he flies!

[Stabs **RUY-GOMEZ**.

RUY-GOMEZ
'Twas aimed well at my heart;
That I had strength enough but to retort!
Dull life, so tamely must I from thee part?
Curses and plagues! revenge, where art thou now?
Meet, meet me at thy own dark house below!

[Dies.

KING
He's gone, and now there's not so vile a thing
As I—

DON JOHN of AUSTRIA
Remember, sir, you are a king.

KING
A king! it is too little: I'll be more,
I tell thee: Nero was an emperor;
He killed his mother, but I've that out-done,
Murdered a loyal wife and guiltless son.
Yet, Austria, why should I grow mad for that?
Is it my fault I was unfortunate?

DON JOHN of AUSTRIA
Collect your spirits, sir, and calm your mind.

KING
Look to't; strange things I tell thee are designed.
Thou, Austria, shalt grow old, and in thy age
Dote, dote, my hero:—oh, a long gray beard,
With eyes distilling rheum, and hollow cheeks,
Will be such charms, thou canst not want success!
But, above all, beware of jealousy;
It was the dreadful curse that ruined me.

DON JOHN of AUSTRIA
Dread sir, no more.

KING
O heart! O Heaven! but stay,
Named I not Heaven? I did, and at the word
(Methought I saw't) the azure fabric stirred.
Oh, for my queen and son the saints prepare;
But I'll pursue and overtake them there;
Whirl, stop the sun, arrest his charioteer;
I'll ride in that: away! pull, pull him down!
Oh, how I'll hurl the wild-fire as I run!
Now, now I mount—

[Runs off raving.

DON JOHN of AUSTRIA
Look to the king.
See of this fair one, too, strict care be had.

[Pointing to **HENRIETTA**.

Despair, how vast a triumph hast thou made!
No more in love's enervate charms I'll lie;
Shaking off softness, to the camp I'll fly,
Where thirst of fame the active hero warms;
And what I've lost in peace, regain in arms.

[Exeunt.

EPILOGUE

Spoken by a **GIRL**.

Now what d'ye think my message hither means?
Yonder's the poet sick behind the scenes:
He told me there was pity in my face,
And therefore sent me here to make his peace.
Let me for once persuade ye to be kind;
For he has promised me to stand my friend;
And if this time I can your kindness move,
He'll write for me, he swears by all above,
When I am big enough to be in love.
Now won't you be good-natured, ye fine men?
Indeed I'll grow as fast as e'er I can,
And try if to his promise he'll be true.
Think on't; when that time comes, you do not know
But I may grow in love with some of you;
Or, at the worst, I'm certain I shall see
Amongst you those who'll swear they're so with me.
But now, if by my suit you'll not be won,—
You know what your unkindness oft has done,—
I'll e'en forsake the play-house, and turn nun.[1]

FOOTNOTES:

[1] This alludes to the retirement of Mrs. Reeves, or, as she was usually termed, Madam Reeves, a very beautiful and accomplished actress, between whom and Dryden there was supposed to be rather too close an intimacy. She withdrew from the stage to a cloister.—Thornton.

THOMAS OTWAY – A SHORT BIOGRAPHY

Thomas Otway was born on March 3rd, 1652 at Trotton near Midhurst, the parish of which his father, Humphrey Otway, was curate.

The family moved to Woolbering, a neighbouring parish, when his father was given the rectorship there and it was here that Otway lived his early years.

He was educated at Winchester College before entering Christ Church, Oxford, in 1669 as a commoner. For reasons unknown he left without a degree in 1672 but what is known is that Oxford create a passion in him for books.

Travelling to London that same year he met and obtained work as an actor from the playwright Aphra Behn. He was cast as the old king in her play, Forc'd Marriage, or The Jealous Bridegroom, at the Dorset Garden Theatre. On his debut he had such a severe attack of stage fright that his acting career finished there and then.

His career now turned to writing plays and it was a career that was to prove of immense worth to the literary canon of England.

In 1675, Thomas Betterton produced, at the Dorset Garden Theatre, Otway's first play, Alcibiades, which was printed in the same year. It is a tragedy, written in heroic verse, saved from absolute failure only by the actors. Elizabeth Barry took the part of Draxilla, and her lover, John Wilmot, 2nd Earl of Rochester, recommended Otway to the Duke of York (later King James II).

Otway became besotted by Elizabeth Barry, and whilst it appears she flirted, and perhaps led him on, she had no wish to upset Wilmot. Otway was to be denied the great love of his life.

His writing however did make great strides. In Don Carlos, Prince of Spain (licensed 15 June 1676). The material for this rhymed tragedy came from the novel of the same name, written in 1672 by the Abbé de Saint-Real. In it the two characters familiar throughout his plays make their appearance. Don Carlos is the impetuous, unstable youth, who seems to be drawn from Otway himself, while the Queen's part is the gentle, pathetic character repeated in his more celebrated heroines, Monimia and Belvidera. It was reported that it was, up to that date, the most successful modern tragedy of the stage.

In 1677 Betterton produced two further adaptations from the French by Otway, Titus and Berenice (from Racine's Bérénice), and the Cheats of Scapin (from Molière's Fourberies de Scapin). These were also printed together, with a dedication to Rochester.

In 1678 Otway produced an original comedy, Friendship in Fashion, which continued his run of very successful plays.

Whilst writing for the stage brought him prestige and money it did not bring the attentions of Elizabeth Barry despite his advances, although she had continued to perform in his plays. There are several letters that he wrote to her that survive, alas they failed to convince her that he was of more benefit than Wilmot was, despite the latter squandering his own talents.

In 1678, driven to desperation, Otway obtained a commission through Charles, Earl of Plymouth, the son of Charles II, in a regiment serving in the Netherlands. The English troops were disbanded in 1679, but were left to find their way home as best they could. They were paid with depreciated paper, and Otway arrived in London late in the year more than disappointed with his lot.

In February 1680, the first of Otway's two tragic masterpieces, The Orphan, or The Unhappy Marriage, was produced at the Dorset Garden, with Elizabeth Barry playing the part of Monimia. Written in blank verse, modelled on that of Shakespeare, its success was due to the tragic pathos, of which Otway was a master, in the characters of Castalio and Monimia. The History and Fall of Caius Marius, produced in the same year, (but only printed in 1692), is a hybrid; grafting Shakespeare's Romeo and Juliet onto the story of Marius as related in Plutarch's Lives.

In 1680 Otway also published The Poets Complaint of his Muse, or A Satyr against Libells, in which he retaliated on his literary enemies.

An indifferent comedy, The Soldier's Fortune (1681), was followed in February 1682 by, perhaps, his best work, Venice Preserv'd, or A Plot Discover'd. Otway's play is based on the Histoire de la conjuration des Espagnols contre la Venise en 1618, also by the Abbé de Saint-Réal. The character of Belvidera is his own, and the leading part in the conspiracy, taken by Bedamor, the Spanish ambassador, is given in the play to the historically insignificant Pierre and Jaffeir.

Venice Preserv'd also contains an allusion to Rochester's famous deathbed conversion, as reported in Gilbert Burnet's Some Passages of the Life and Death of... Rochester (1680). The conversion was doubted by many, and Otway is obviously sceptical, for when Pierre is on the scaffold, attended by a priest, he is made to say the following to his executioner (Act V, Scene II): "Captain, I'd have hereafter / This fellow write no Lies of my Conversion."

The play won instant success. It was translated into all the significant European languages. The great Dryden said of it: "Nature is there, which is the greatest beauty."

The Orphan and Venice Preserv'd continued to remain stock pieces of the stage until the 19th century.

Otway's last and most obscure play is The Atheist (1684), although many see it as a way to cash in on his previous comic success with The Soldier's Fortune, it is seen as either a weak sequel or a brilliant experiment. One of the play's ambitions is to show what happens after the wedding as sentimental conclusion in plays of the period through the figures of Courtine and Sylvia. The bleakness of their relations taint those of Beauregard and Porcia. The complexity of the plot, some of which derives from the "Invisible Mistress," the first interpolated story in Paul Scarron's Roman comique, speak of the maze of human life, a meaningless world left for the audience to decipher. One or two prefaces, and two posthumous pieces, a poem, Windsor Castle (1685), a panegyric of Charles II, and a History of the Triumvirates (1686), translated from the French, complete the list of Otway's works.

However, in the last few years of his life poverty had ensnared Otway. The success of his earlier plays had finished with Venice Preserv'd and the downward slope was both precipitous and destructive.

The generally accepted story regarding the manner of his death was first given in Theophilus Cibber's Lives of the Poets. He is said to have emerged from his retreat at the Bull on Tower Hill to beg for bread. A passer-by, learning who he was, gave him a guinea, with which Otway hastened to a baker's shop. He ate too hastily, and choked on the first mouthful. It may be true, it may be not but that he died in the most awful poverty on April 14th, 1685 is certain. Thomas Otway was buried two days later on April 16th, in the churchyard of St. Clement Danes.

THOMAS OTWAY – A CONCISE BIBLIOGRAPHY

Alcibiades (1675)
In Don Carlos, Prince of Spain (1676)
Titus and Berenice (from Racine's Bérénice) (1677)
Cheats of Scapin (from Molière's Fourberies de Scapin) (1677)
Friendship in Fashion (1678)
The Orphan, or The Unhappy Marriage (1680)
The History and Fall of Caius Marius (1680)
The Poets Complaint of his Muse, or A Satyr against Libells (1680)
The Soldier's Fortune (1681)
Venice Preserv'd, or A Plot Discover'd (1682)
The Atheist (1684)

www.ingramcontent.com/pod-product-compliance
Lightning Source LLC
Chambersburg PA
CBHW060140050426
42448CB00010B/2222